RESEARCH IN TEAMS

# RESEARCH IN TEAMS
## A PRACTICAL GUIDE TO GROUP POLICY ANALYSIS

Custom Edition for the University of Phoenix

**Dan Bednarz**
*University of Pittsburgh*
*Katz Graduate School of Business*

**Donna J. Wood**
*University of Pittsburgh*
*Katz Graduate School of Business*

SIMON & SCHUSTER CUSTOM PUBLISHING

*Research in Teams: A Practical Guide to Group Policy Analysis*, by Dan Bednarz and Donna J. Wood
Copyright © 1991 by Prentice-Hall, Inc.
A Simon & Schuster Company
Englewood Cliffs, New Jersey 07632


This special edition published in cooperation with
Simon & Schuster Custom Publishing

Printed in the United States of America

10 9 8 7 6 5 4 3 2 1

ISBN 0–536–59366-3
BA 95096

 **SIMON & SCHUSTER CUSTOM PUBLISHING**

160 Gould St./Needham Heights, MA 02194
Simon & Schuster Education Group

# CONTENTS

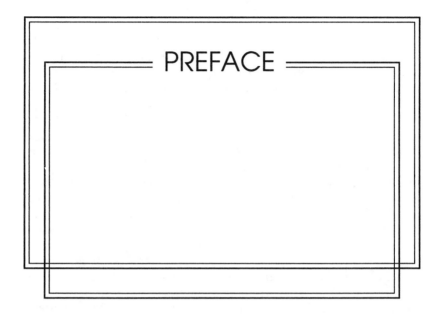

# PREFACE

This is a guidebook on the structure and dynamics of team-based policy analysis (public policy or business policy—also known as *strategic management*).  It provides detailed instruction on how to research and prepare an analysis while simultaneously covering the group dynamics of team-based projects.  It is designed for a wide range of people:  from those who are unsure whether they know anything about policy analysis and teamwork, to those who know a great deal about them yet are seeking to make their efforts more efficient and effective and their product more organized, thorough, and creative.  Consequently, we assume little about our readers other than that: (1) they are intelligent and motivated, (2) they are willing to work as a team preparing a policy analysis, and (3) the team will in some sense operate democratically.

We write in reaction to three common but unfortunate patterns that detract from such team efforts.  First, we help readers overcome the quick-and-dirty approach to policy analysis. Although there are tradeoffs between available time and the quality of the product rendered, it is incorrect to assume an inverse relationship where the quicker one does the job, the dirtier it must be.  Once one dons the quick-and-dirty hat, poor, inaccurate, and perhaps worthless or dishonest work is the likely result. Moreover, when a team enjoys and is proud of what it is doing, it invariably uses its time to better effect. In essence, here we show how it is possible to do a quick-and-clean analysis.

A second pattern is that students assigned group policy work frequently flounder on elemental questions that they are inhibited to pose lest they seem dumb or poorly trained. It is common for students to fret— and rightly so— over questions like: what are my rights and responsibilities as a team member? where do we start? how do we start? what is a policy analysis, anyway? where do we look for information? what is the assigned question really asking? how can we best use our time to organize the report?  These are not dumb questions; they are what beginners need to know, and it is often difficult— on pain of social and intellectual embarrassment— for beginners to get these critical questions answered so that they can get to the heart of the project. Given this, a major challenge in writing this book is to accommodate the wide range of baselines from which readers begin.  Here we take a "where's the on/off switch" or "for the completely uninformed" approach (that is, no question is too obvious), and then offer a guide to the stages and procedures involved in assembling and presenting a public policy or strategy analysis. As presented, the readers decide which sections of our book to learn from or to pass over as familiar ground.

The final and critically important pattern that troubles us is the individual's seemingly natural dread of teamwork, which is especially felt since the reward (for students— a grade) is not wholly within one's control.  A team is built from persons who probably are fearful of losing some of their autonomy and sense of self-control to the group.  In time, however, they learn that by directing their competitive juices to the project and engaging in a cooperative effort with one another— based on their trust of the group— they will successfully complete the assigned task. With an understanding of group dynamics and team-building processes, supplemented by illustrations from our teaching experiences, team members will be able to cope with the myriad issues that affect a team's performance.

Furthermore, we believe that teams have formidable strengths not widely appreciated; indeed, learning to work with a group is itself a vital skill for professionals to attain. We therefore point out how teamwork can greatly benefit individual members; as compared to an individual, teams usually have a variety of talents, skills, and advantages in at least the following areas: (1) range of expertise and knowledge of the issue, (2) depth of analysis, creativity, and insights, (3) writing and speaking skills, (4) number of hours to devote to the project, and (5) the speed with which the project can be completed.

This book can do a great deal for team members; it will examine the major intellectual hurdles, the grunt work, and the group processes involved when several individuals, presumably from three to eight persons, form a team to do a policy analysis.

The book is structured so that task-oriented and people-oriented issues are addressed together. Because of the critical difference between a group project and a mere composite of individual efforts, we first turn in Chapter 1 to a consideration of teamwork, followed in Chapter 2 by some introductory comments on policy analysis and the formats used in the issue-brief projects. In Chapter 3, we return to the team— its members and its issues, especially communication and conflict. Chapter 4 shows how to resolve common problems encountered in dealing with the research topic, and Chapters 5 and 6 detail the process of doing a literature search and working with published data sources. Interviewing, obtaining information from human sources, is the subject of Chapter 7. Chapter 8 takes up the vital question of analysis— what it is, how to do it. In Chapter 9 the process of writing the brief and constructing bibliographic references is covered, and Chapter 10 examines the issues and possibilities in the oral presentation. Chapter 11 offers instruction on how to assess the team process itself— the problems you encountered, how they were handled, and the actual outputs of the team's efforts.

## *Acknowledgments*

Over the years, our students at Vanderbilt University, the University of Michigan, Slippery Rock University, and the University of Pittsburgh conducted issue-brief research on an enormous variety of topics, and taught us how it should be done. Sheila Tobias gave us the idea in the first place. Dr. Susan Neumann and Dennis Smith of the Katz Graduate School of Business Library, University of Pittsburgh, proved that librarians really know their stuff, and helped enormously in the basic

research.  Our Apple Macintoshes made the writing and rewrit-
ing a great deal more pleasant and easier than it could have
been.  The Wissenschaftszentrum Berlin für Sozialforschung
provided the time and space we needed to finish the manuscript.
We thank our editor at Prentice Hall, Alison Reeves, and also
Kerry Reardon and Audrey Kopciak for their assistance in seeing
this book through the publishing process.  Corinne Nagy, a
student at Tufts University, read and edited the manuscript for
us, saying at the end, "I know how to do a policy analysis now."
In the hope that they will find it equally helpful, we dedicate this
book to the students who read and use it.

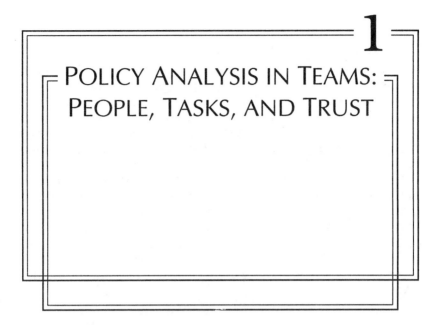

# POLICY ANALYSIS IN TEAMS: PEOPLE, TASKS, AND TRUST

You looked over the syllabus and groaned. "Another group project!" Subdued murmurs ran through the class. Students started looking around to identify prospective teammates in case memberships were self-selected. You kept reading. "Policy analysis," you muttered, "in groups, yet." And off you went to get this handbook.

More and more, in undergraduate, graduate, and professional schools and programs as well as some social science programs, students are being required to combine policy research and analysis with group dynamics skills. More often than not, however, students are taught a fair amount about policy but not very much about group dynamics. Even students who have taken a class in organizational behavior, group psychology, or team building, may not have much of an idea about how to actually apply what they have learned to accomplishing a group research project.

The reasons for doing policy-based research are clear: business and professional students are constantly affected by the policy decisions of private organizations and government bodies, and it is important that they know how to analyze policies and relate them to specific job-related situations. The reasons for doing group work in school are equally well established. Instructors expect students to learn how to manage themselves in teams, how to apply their behavioral science understandings to real situations, how to allocate tasks and monitor completion, and how to produce a whole product from the various pieces of each person's contribution. These are valuable skills in the real world, where teamwork now accounts for a vast number of projects in business and the professions.

In this book you will learn something about doing policy analysis, and you will learn something about managing in groups. More importantly, you will learn how to work through the various stages of a team-researched policy analysis project without sacrificing either the analysis or the team. In the process, you should have a richer, more productive learning experience, and you may even discover some skills you didn't know you had.

## THE ISSUE BRIEF—NOT JUST A TERM PAPER

In this book you will learn how a team can use its collective resources to do a policy analysis, called an *issue brief,* either in public policy or strategic management. This type of research and policy issue brief is distinct from academic or student term-paper research because it is focused on a concise summary and analysis of a significant public policy issue, not just a review of what the issue is, or who said what, when, about the issue. The policy-issue brief requires that a great amount of information, analysis, and argument be packed into a relatively short document. Clearly, this calls for a sound command of the issue.

As we present it, the police-issue brief has two main results: (1) an oral presentation, and (2) a written, tightly argued, and well-supported briefing document on the policy issue. The format is designed to serve professionals or to prepare students for the conditions under which most professional policy analyses are done: the need to allocate scarce time, working in a team, conducting research in unconventional as well as conventional ways, critically sifting through and weighing large amounts of evidence, considering several policy options, and preparing a concise, persuasive oral and written presentation with policy recommendations.

The format we present in the subsequent chapters has a natural history to it in that teams proceed through several phases, each with its distinctive problems, challenges, and pleasures. The chapters are organized in terms of this natural history so that they reflect how the team actually proceeds rather than an idealized version of how the team should proceed. Before we move to the format, however, we will briefly explore the other side of the issue-brief coin— the fact that the research is conducted by a team.

## TEAMWORK: TRUST AND CONTRACTS

A team is a special kind of group that forms to work towards a common purpose, but it takes effort to make a gathering of individuals into a team that will succeed at that common purpose. Successful teams have members who trust one another and share a sense of group identity. Accordingly, they develop a contractlike relationship, based on that trust, which gives purpose, operating standards, rules, and direction to the team. Before discussing these core elements of the successful team in detail, we will mention the general stereotypes about groups— that is, teams and committees— that are impediments to individual achievements and productivity.

One of the most formidable obstacles to teamwork is the belief of individuals that joining forces with others will harm their own interests. Most of us have heard the jokes about committees or teams and how they often misconstrue simple directions, make enormous problems of little issues, or devise Rube Goldberg-like (or, for those of a younger generation, Pee-Wee Herman-like) solutions for straightforward matters. In American society, where individual achievement and competition are strongly extolled values, it is easy to disdain or be suspicious about working in a task-oriented group (a team or a committee) because the group is viewed as imposing needless constraints or exploitative circumstances on the individual. In addition, one often hears that groups: smother creativity; come up with banal, watered down, or impractical solutions; work slowly; and are beset with free riders or laggard members who take the credit while one or two diligent members actually do all the work.

Despite the jokes, which indicate widely held beliefs, it is in teams and committees that the majority of organizational work gets done. One well-known management study found, for example, that top level corporate managers spend more than half of their time in meetings where joint efforts are applied to managerial concerns.[1] And the research is clear in showing that it is typically in groups that the best and most creative problem solving is done. If you consider the complexity and specialization of the late twentieth-century world, it is not difficult to see why so many problems are assigned to teams, where differing experiences, expertise, and styles of thinking and problem solving can be combined to advantage.

Professionals of all kinds regularly find themselves working in groups (such as teams, task forces, or committees). For students studying to join a profession, the interpersonal experience gained from working in a team is equally as valuable as the intellectual experience of doing a policy analysis. That is, knowing how to work with people in a team setting is a valued skill of professionals.

Groups as such, then, are really not a hindrance but a boon to problem solving. The research on group-based problem solving amply shows that in virtually all instances it is a rare individual who can match a group's performance. This research and our experiences also show that success is most often found in groups where trust among members is high and provides the basis for a contract-like relationship to exist. We will come back to this in a moment, but first let us discuss what a team is.

A *team* is a specific type of group that has *people engaged in a joint, cooperative effort to accomplish a specified task or goal that one person cannot do or would find very difficult to do.* Assuming they have the appropriate skills and resources, several persons willing to *trust* in each other, that is, *team-up*, will be more successful at their task than any of them would be working alone.

The central dynamic tension of the team, then, is that individuals must cooperate and coordinate their efforts—and trust enough to become a team— to achieve a collective goal any one of them could not, or would find hard to accomplish alone. Does this call for each member to give away some individual competitiveness and autonomy to the group? Of course, but we all do this in virtually every aspect of our lives anyway; it is called give-and-take or cooperation. The question is not *if* but *how much* and *what kind* of competitiveness and autonomy we give up. Equally important, it is a question about what we gain from the exchange. If all goes well, what we gain is a smoothly functioning team that accomplishes the task, where each member can rely on the other members to do their part, with the result a better product from which all can benefit.

The misconceptions and negative feelings about teams and committees probably stem from a combination of our cultural emphasis on the triumphant individual unencumbered by the group—the Clint Eastwood icon, for example—and the real problems that can arise in joint efforts. In the U.S., we do appear to have a cultural myth that idolizes lone cowboy-heroes, and maybe there isn't much we can do about it except to acknowledge it and try to discern its effects on our behavior.

Regarding the real problems of groups, however, consider that one or two members bent on disrupting the group usually can do some damage to it. Consider further that being a member of a group does not mean that one has no other conflicting group memberships; a person may join a group just to make sure it fails so that another group will triumph. These Machiavellian maneuvers are only pointed out to show how bad the inefficiency and ineffectiveness of teams can get. With some careful thought, observation, and action, your team can avoid such stereotypes and games and can illustrate just how good and productive a group effort can be.

## THREE PARTS OF A TEAM CONTRACT: TASKS, DIVISION OF LABOR, AND RULES

We have already indicated that trust among members is crucial to a successful team project. A trusting team feels—pick your term—cohesiveness, solidarity, a "we feeling," a general sense of cooperativeness, a sense of belonging, or a group identity. Competition is friendly and is channelled to the success of the team, not exclusively to the success of any one team member. That is, members have a collective purpose where the success of the group is sought by each member as the primary goal, and each individual's interests are tied positively to the group, not in opposition or indifference to it. This is not always easy to accomplish (and we give attention to this matter directly throughout the book), since there is a tendency for individuals, especially students who are concerned with their own grades, to think of themselves at the expense of the group. (For instance: "What's in it for me? How little can I get away with doing? I'd better be cautious because they will take advantage of me. How can I make myself look good while not giving up too much of my energy and time?")

Many philosophers and social scientists have shown us in their discussions of the *prisoners' dilemma*, however, that teamwork is the best solution for all involved. Prisoners' dilemma games take many specific forms, but the basic idea is a challenge: should one act for one's own interests or those of the group? When contextual elements and human relationships are taken into account, the answer is that acting in the group's interests normally works out to the individual's advantage.

The most successful teams we have encountered in our teaching unanimously note in their debriefings or project evaluations that expressions and acts of individual competitiveness and selfishness— not disagreement, a distinctly different thing— were minimal or absent in the team, or appeared only at the beginning of the project. As many students put it, "everyone just pulled together and got it done." Conversely, the poor results we have gotten from teams usually are traced not to the intellectual deficiencies of the members, but to a prolonged lack of group trust, which inhibits the ability to create a sense of common purpose and makes members unable to see their personal goals (a grade, doing a high-quality job, and looking competent in public) as best served through the actions of the group. This failure to establish a group identity, in essence a team, goes hand in hand with poor team results.

To recapitulate, the basis of a well-functioning team is the members' belief that they can trust all members to do their parts in attaining the common purpose (here, the policy analysis) of the group. As a foundation of trust is established, the team's identity develops around a shared, detailed understanding of how the task is to be done, how the members will share the work, and finally, the rules under which they will operate. We will discuss these topics separately but keep in mind that they are most likely to develop in unison with each other, as part of an entire conception of the team.

A few more words about trust are in order, since some may take it to mean that team members have a right to seek personal information about members, or that members should be able to trust each other in all things. The trust required in a task-oriented team is of a limited and specific kind; you need only trust that the members will act professionally and do their share of work on the policy analysis according to the rules of the assignment as well as those the group establishes. Even if you do not like a fellow member, you may nonetheless be confident, under all but the most strained conditions, that the member will fulfill any obligations to the team. That is what professionalism and trust mean in this context: we have a job to do regardless of our personal feelings for one another.

In essence, then, the task-oriented team is based on trust and a contract. Whether the contract is oral or written is a matter for team consideration; the team should not, however, have an implicit (that is, unstated or vague) contract. Implicit contracts may not be contracts at all because they are subject to multiple interpretations of the task, division of labor, and rules. These different understandings can guide team members' efforts to the very end, when they discover that they have not been working toward the same objectives after all. This is a situation a team wants to avoid as it would the plague. As a process of team formation, there must be an open discussion about the elements of the contract, and the contract should be reviewed as frequently as the progress of the work and changing views of the members require.

Therefore, as task-oriented teams build trust among their members, they actually are forming a contractual bond about how to complete the task, presumably because no reasonable person enters into a contract without believing that it will be honored or enforced.

The common features of a team contract are a task (the policy analysis), a division of labor, and team rules. A contract is a shared agreement which includes these elements and points to how the entire policy analysis process will be handled. Let's consider each of these in turn as to their importance for the team.

## The Task

The research on teams suggests that to perform well, teams must develop a collective understanding of and focus on their task. That seems obvious, except when we realize that team members may have distracting commitments on their time or distracting relationships with one another: co-worker, friend, roommate, lover, rival, and so on. On occasion, a team must actively work to control these distractions because their time together and their collective energy are scarce. We have seen a few teams where goofing off, commiserating, or discussing members' personal and social lives were the focus of group activities, while the policy analysis was a secondary concern; and in a few instances we have seen teams that rarely met at all because of other "more important things to do."

Regarding socializing, or just plain shooting the bull, a team does not have to rule out such nontask activities entirely because, in a moderate amount, they will likely contribute to team cohesiveness. But team members should understand that most of the team's energy and time are to be spent getting down to business. Successful teams establish a pattern where work is primary, and joking, playing, or personal discussions may take place, but do not take over.

As the team forms, an outline of rules concerning the task focus should emerge from consideration of such basic matters as these: what will be accomplished at each meeting, how often meetings will occur, each member's responsibility to come prepared and to do assigned work, and rules for fighting (resolving conflict or differences).

Agreement on the scope and method for doing the task must never be taken for granted. It is crucial for the team to pay conscious attention to the formation of a *consensus* on what the task is, how much effort it will take to do a high-quality job (which, by the way, should not be taken for granted as a goal of each member), the steps necessary to do the job and, most of all, on how much effort each member thinks the project requires. True, you cannot know all of this precisely at the beginning of the project, so as they are needed, the team must hold discussions. Yet a discussion of the assignment as the team first forms is very important, no matter how vague the task may seem initially.

At this point a beginner might ask: "Why should you make sure that a consensus is reached about the assignment (task)? Isn't it obvious what has to be done?"

Actually, it is not obvious at all. It is heartbreaking for team members to have a confrontation far into the project where one member huffily says to an accusatory or exasperated fellow member: "Well, I don't see it that way at all, you seem to take this too seriously and want to put more time into it than I do. I've got other classes to worry about, too." Once the actual work has begun, it is more difficult to alter such differences over the task. Two contrary definitions of the project have clashed belatedly, and the psychological commitments of members to their positions are now difficult to change. Additionally, people may have honest differences over what the specifics of the task are and how to divide their efforts, differences that are best uncovered and resolved as soon as they are discovered, and certainly before much work is done on the policy analysis.

We have found that almost any disagreement over the scope of the task is negotiable in the team formation stage, but as time goes on, and work is done, commitments tend to harden and negotiation becomes more difficult. In extreme cases, instead of coming together as a team for the final analysis and presentation, the team begins to weaken because of an underlying conflict over its task, with the oral presentation and written report reflecting the discord no matter how much the members try to disguise it. (Parenthetically for now, we mention that the policy issue-brief format we present later explicitly provides for differences of opinion among the members in the form of majority and dissenting minority reports. This legitimizes genuine disagreements and turns them away from power struggles and towards an intellectual challenge to state one's case reasonably and forcefully.)

Attention to the task definition, as a part of the overall contract discussion, serves not only to bring to the surface and then settle differences among members, it also serves in the team formation process. As members argue, negotiate, agree or disagree, they are learning about one another as they move toward a working consensus on the task. From these kinds of discussions about the scope of the task, trust and group identity are built, and a contractual relationship begins to take shape.

## Division of Labor

Discussions on the division of labor are equally important to building trust and group identity and they add to the development of the team's contract. The advantages of dividing the labor are apparent, since it is possible for a team to accomplish much more work than an individual. Also, members usually have complementary skills and different styles of thinking that make straightforward or interesting for one member what would be difficult drudgery for another.

The fundamental point about dividing the labor is that it cannot be divorced from the trust issue. Members should have a good idea of their assignments, and there should be agreement that the work is divided in a way that is acceptable to all members. It would be arbitrary and useless for us to try to lay out any precise terms regarding what is an acceptable division of labor; each team must come to its own decision. The critical factors, however, are these:

1. That the team members believe the divisions they have made are fair, by some standard acceptable to all.
2. That no alterations of standards and assignments are made without group discussion and consensus (no private side deals).

Towards this end, it is helpful for members to talk in turn about the assignments in relation to their skills and to suggest parts of the work that they would like to do. This may seem difficult or even pointless at the beginning of the project, when so much is unknown about the task, but do it anyway because what you learn about group members the first time around will be of value the second, third, and subsequent times you consider dividing the work, when the picture of what needs to be done is much sharper.

Out of this initial division of labor will come a better understanding of the capabilities of each member and a better sense of the team's overall abilities, skills, and potential. (And from discussions of the task, trust and group identity continue to build up.) For example, it is common for one of the members to reveal something previously unmentioned, such as a skill or work experience directly relevant to the assignment. (In fact, we have noticed that many students choose a research topic because of knowledge or experience they have had.)

In an area as sensitive as dividing the labor, be certain that too vocal or domineering types— discussed more below as normal members of a team— do not take over and hand out assignments suiting only their interests. Be certain, too, that quiet members actually talk in detail, not just mutter or nod in acceptance about whether or not they think the assignments are fair. In this way, it is hard for disgruntled or concerned quiet members to disguise their genuine reactions, and perhaps to blow up about equity issues later on in the policy analysis process. As with the task element, talking about, elaborating on, arguing over, and negotiating the division of labor adds to the trust of the members and contributes to the formation of the team's contract. Above all else, the motto is that early establishment of *what's fair* should not be glossed over. If this glossing over takes place, the team risks later destructive conflict over equity issues.

Considering the division of labor brings up the significant matter of team leadership. Few topics are so widely studied and so little understood as leadership. For our purposes, we suggest that the group avoid the *do we need a leader?* question, and instead deal with generic team issues usually associated with the idea of leadership. These issues, listed below, are all part of the division of labor and naturally raise the question of who decides how and when these activities are done:

1. The allocation of team resources.
2. The assignment of roles or work.
3. Keeping track of the overall direction of the project.
4. Keeping up team motivation and morale.
5. Planning and strategy for doing and presenting the analysis to the public (that is, those relevant parties outside of the team).

We assume that the team operates on democratic principles, although this does not tell you much about team leadership except that you do not want arbitrary dictators running teams strictly to serve their interests. Democratic leadership may mean that every decision must be ratified or made by the entire group, or it may mean that the group is consulted by an elected

leader about decisions, or it may mean that specific responsibilities are delegated to certain members by the group for action
and reporting back.

In a small task-oriented group it is not inevitable for one
person to step forth, be acclaimed the leader, and to take on all
leadership responsibilities. Nor is it always desirable. Some
groups will do very well reaching consensus on every major
decision and then delegating responsibilities and roles on an ad
hoc basis. In other groups, one person indeed may emerge as
the leader and take on all major responsibilities, to the satisfaction of all. In still other teams, the leadership role may shift from
person to person, depending on the situation or needs confronting the group (for example, today the team is down and needs
morale building and motivation; tomorrow the team may be
going full steam and need evaluation and guidance; the next day
the team may be confused and need a firm hand to draw it back
to the task). Your team will develop its own sense of itself and
each member's competencies, and will come to know which
approach works best. An advantage of small groups is that
several answers to the leadership question are available.

**Team Rules**

Team rules easily arise out of the team's previous discussions
of the task and its division of labor. The rules both contribute
to and reinforce team unity and the view of the members that
as individuals their best interests lie in serving the team, not in
exploiting it. In the outstanding teams we have seen, as well as
from the research on teams, we learn that members feel a
responsibility to one another similar to, but obviously not as
intense as that felt towards one's family or friends. A cardinal
rule of the team therefore is not to act in one's self-interest if
doing so will hurt the team. Of course it is incumbent on the
group members to support one another and to demonstrate that
in actuality all individuals' interests are safe, secure, and well
served in the team.

Rules also refer to procedural matters such as the way
meetings are run, penalties for members who miss team meetings and for those who do not do their assigned tasks or do them
poorly, codes of conduct in meetings, and especially methods of

arguing and conflict resolution. (More will be said on these important topics later.)

For some teams, drawing up written rules about these topics will seem silly or a waste of time, and we are sympathetic with that reaction. However, some teams find it valuable to write down a simple set of rules, especially if members know each other slightly and thus have expectations but little knowledge of each other's abilities and work styles.

Whether rules are written down is something for each team to think about and decide; but in any case, the rules must be shared and understood by all team members. A general understanding of what is and is not allowed of team members should be developed early in team meetings. Without this understanding, confusion over the scope of the task, assignments, rules, rights and responsibilities is likely to occur at high-anxiety or high-uncertainty points in the research process. If the other elements, task definition and division of labor, have been dealt with satisfactorily, the rules should develop naturally or with a little thinking through on the part of the team.

A word of caution is needed. We are covering team building in a logical manner, and the reader might conclude that to have a successful team, each aspect we discuss must be explicitly addressed by the team. This is not so; our intent is to make you aware of what is involved in team building so that you will have some sense of the issues facing your team. This discussion is not a prescription for a successful team; it is a perspective that you can bring to your team-building efforts. The manner in which teams build trust and establish a contractual relationship varies, and what we point out is that successful teams do have trust and a contractual relationship.

Some teams will develop what feels like an instant rapport among their members. There will be much agreement, little apparent conflict, and a great deal of self-satisfaction about how easy this group research really is. Some team members take an instant dislike to each other, or carry into a team dislikes already formed, with resulting hostility, stalling, and verbal aggression. In most cases, however, team members will need to build rapport through discussion and the resolution of disagreements. The negotiated solution can be just as viable— in some cases more so— as the instantaneous love feast.

## Consulting the Instructor
## on Task-Related Problems

On the matter of the struggles your team may be having with some aspect of the work, for example, your initial problem analysis or where to look for information or how to divide the labor, a conversation with the instructor can be of immense value *after* you have made an effort to solve the matter within the team. Remember that instructors' experience and expertise in group processes and policy analysis should allow them to see things you do not see; and as outside parties they are not as likely to suffer from the forest-or-trees problem of being so immersed in projects that it is hard to gain an overall picture of them. Finally, instructors are not going to be feeling anxious about the project, and you and your teammates probably are; such collective anxiety can introduce impasses, stubbornness, and blind spots into your team.

The general rule to go by is that if you can honestly say you are stumped and you have tried to resolve the trouble within the team with little or no result, then you should seek the advice of the instructor. Do not go to the instructor as a first step, since this can lead to a dependence which is counterproductive to what you can learn from the project, or even worse, a denial of help later when you really need it. None of this implies that the instructor does not want to see you or that you are in a sink-or-swim position. Push your team to its limits in solving problems and if unsuccessful, then consult the instructor. Finally, you don't have enough time to put problems off, and your final product will likely suffer if you try it.


*CONCLUSION*

In this chapter we covered an introduction to team-based policy analysis and delved into the critical aspects of how teams get started and how they develop a sense of trust that allows them to work in a contractlike relationship. Problem-focused teams are already regular features in organizations, and considering the increasing interdependence of modern life, they are likely to become even more prevalent, as they offer significant advantages over what one person can accomplish. The ability to work in teams on policy-analysis tasks, then, is a valuable skill for professionals.

## *ENDNOTES*

1. Henry Mintzberg, *The Nature of Managerial Work* (New York: Harper & Row), 1973.

# 2

# POLICY ANALYSIS
# AND THE
# ISSUE BRIEF FORMATS

At the outset we promised to deal with those "dumb" questions that students often have but are afraid to ask. We understand that guidebooks often assume that readers already know what in fact they are seeking to find out! For those who are unfamiliar, therefore, we first discuss what policy analysis *is*, and then introduce the formats for the team-researched public-policy and strategic-management issue briefs.

## *POLICY ANALYSIS—WHAT IS IT?*

What is a *policy*? Very simply put, a policy is a course of action. It is a more or less integrated set of decisions taken over a period of time. A policy also connotes the way things are done, as in: "It's our policy not to exchange a video game if the package seal is broken," or, "It's our policy to exchange unsatisfactory merchandise with no questions asked." In formal planning terms, a policy is a written statement intended to guide practice, a declaration of what should be done under certain circumstances.

What is *analysis*? Analysis refers to studying the essential nature of something by examining what its various components are, and how these parts work and fit together. Combine these concepts and you have something more than the sum of its parts— *policy analysis.*

A dean of a school of public policy has said that he discourages his graduate students from thinking too deeply about what policy analysis is, since it is such a multifaceted and perplexing question that it usually serves merely to bore them.[1] It is not that he does not believe in policy analysis, however, because he himself is one of the foremost practitioners of the art. Policy analysis plays a fundamental role in modern society because so many people— politicians, educators, business leaders, and just plain folk— believe there is a relationship between *what we know* (knowledge) and *what we do* (action). In its most minimal and comprehensive sense, policy analysis is about producing or assessing knowledge and information that can inform our decisions and actions.

Although anyone can come up with qualifications and perhaps outright challenges to this notion of the connection between knowledge and future action, it is what underlies and justifies policy analysis. Some knowledge, no matter its shortcomings, is almost always superior to no knowledge, especially when you are considering how to allocate resources (money, time, building space, health care benefits, or whatever) for future events. If we study and think about what has taken place, we should be able to learn what to do in the future.

We can now offer a proper definition: *policy analysis is a formal, research-based attempt to gather and assess information to create new knowledge bearing on a specific issue (or set of related issues) that requires a decision about allocating resources.* It goes without saying that, all other things being equal, the better the policy analysis, the better the understanding of the policy options and the policy decision. Note that this means that appropriate information and assessments are available to guide decision making. It does not mean that a better decision will result, for political and business decisions are made for all sorts of reasons.

In this chapter we outline the formats for developing a public-policy issue brief and its private-sector cousin, a strategic-management or business-policy issue brief. Both types of policy analysis proceed on the premise that knowledge is indispensable to policy and decision making. Both types of policy research, accordingly, address problems and the options available to solve them; and both are vitally concerned with how scarce resources, either public or private, are to be allocated.

One definition of public policy is that it is the social allocation of values or, put simply, how society (usually through the mechanisms of government) spends its money and other resources. For example, a state has only so much money available for public expenditures such as education, road maintenance, health care, and aid to the poor. The fact that these activities receive state funding and attention indicates that they are socially valued. To use a sharp counterexample, pornography normally does not receive state funding, except to prosecute purveyors— implying that it is negatively valued by society, that is, resources are allocated to control or prevent it. Without oversimplifying too much, the *amount* of money spent in these areas is one reflection of *how much* social value is placed on them; some areas will get more funding, others less. (Of course, officials will always tell disappointed or disgruntled advocates of one or another area that they would like to spend more but cannot because of a lack of funds.) The government, in essence, allocates values, as these values are primarily but not fully expressed through its allotment of funds in the budget.

Similarly, a private firm has a budget that reflects its allocation of corporate values. Does the firm believe strongly in the need for research and development so that new products can be created? If so, R and D will be a major portion of the budget. Does the company value tried-and-true products and see no need for large outlays on research and development? If so, marketing may be more heavily favored. Does the firm place strong emphasis on the design of its products? Does it value its staff and spend time and money on developing their abilities and gaining their loyalty to the firm? How an organization budgets its resources will tell us a great deal about what it values and considers important.

In addition to telling us *what is*, both public-policy and strategic-management analysis are useful in helping us determine *what may be* and *what can be*. At its best, policy analysis involves forecasting— ways of imagining, intuiting, mathematically projecting, and betting on possible futures— so that decision makers can come up with the best way to use scarce resources. This brings us back to the link between knowledge and action: to arrive at a better understanding of how things are, how they are changing, and how they might come to be is a central aim of public-policy or strategic-management analysis. The issue brief format, presented below, is a good way to move toward achievement of this aim.

## *THE ISSUE BRIEF: AN OVERVIEW*

As we outline it, a public-policy issue brief is a tightly constructed, comprehensive, analytic statement on the background and current status of some legal, political, ethical, economic, or social issue. It includes a critical account and consideration of the positions and actions of the interest groups (or *stakeholders*) that support or oppose various policy options, and the team's own analysis and synthesis of available pertinent information, all of which will be the basis of its policy recommendations.

A strategic-management issue brief is similar to its public-policy counterpart with these important differences: it typically focuses on the strategy of a *particular* firm operating within an industry where there is an array of contingencies that affect the firm in formulating its strategy. Depending on the circumstances, these contingencies may include: environmental trends, conditions, opportunities, threats; and organizational features such as culture, structure, history, resources, and leadership.

## *COMPONENTS OF THE PUBLIC-POLICY ISSUE BRIEF*

The components of a public-policy and a strategic-management issue brief are obviously not identical. In this section we present the public-policy issue brief format, followed in the next section by the format for the strategic-management issue brief. The formal structure of a public-policy issue brief is as shown in Figure 2.1, although it may be modified given the nature of the issue or the pedagogical aims of the instructor. Remember, this is the format for the written issue brief *and* an outline for an oral presentation.

In the sections below, these components are discussed briefly. In subsequent chapters we revisit each component in

---

**FIGURE 2.1 Outline for a Public-Policy Issue Brief**

1. Issue Definition
2. Policy Background
3. Specific History of the Issue
4. Stakeholder/Interest Group Analysis
5. Disinterested (Society's) Policy Recommendations
6. Interest-Based Policy Recommendations
7. Bibliography
8. Appendices (optional, as needed)

---

greater depth as we follow your team through its research process.

## 1. Issue Definition

A short statement of the issue being examined is needed to introduce and set up the body (the main research and analytical portions) of the issue brief. Describing the issue at hand seems deceptively simple until you try to put down, in a paragraph or two, how your team defines and will address the issue.

The definition of the issue given in the issue brief, orally and in writing, must be concise and clear so that intelligent readers or listeners (your audience) will have a good grasp of what you are about to offer them and why you think it's important and relevant. If you do not make contact with the audience here, on the first page, you probably won't be in touch with it as you proceed through the report. If you understand what your team discovered and concluded about your issue, here is the place to prove it to others.

Let's look quickly at some of the problems that can arise in coming up with a good issue definition statement.

*Shifting definitions.* Often teams do not really know what the issue is until they have finished researching and analyzing it. Team members feel that the issue has several sides that keep shifting focus as each new bit of information is uncovered or each stage of analysis proceeds. This is perfectly normal, although unsettling! As you go along, you always should have a working conception of the issue, no matter how confused or how different from yesterday's, and compare it to the original issue definition with which you began. This process allows you to see how the issue shifts focus as you learn more about it, and helps you keep track of which issue is driving your research.

*Switching issues.* Sometimes the definition of an issue shifts so much during the course of research that you present a paper on a topic far different from the one with which you started. This may happen because of a poor initial definition, because the issue actually does change as a public-policy drama unfolds in current events, or because the initial definition was a good starting place but could not be sustained. Keep asking if you are still studying the same issue you began with, and if not, do you have solid grounds for your shift? You may want to let the professor know how your issue is being altered as you go along, since this can protect you (and the professor) from unwelcome surprises when the report is submitted. After going through a lengthy research process, you certainly don't want to hear: "This is not the topic I assigned to you!" Also, the professor may be able to help you sort out your issue if you feel that your team is stuck or confused in defining it.

*Mammoth issue.* It is not uncommon for a topic to be too immense for one team to handle. If you start out studying government regulation, it may sound neat and confined, but when you attempt to manage this monster, you find that there are literally hundreds of thousands of government documents, books, and articles on an immense range of regulatory topics. Indeed, some clever instructors may assign a hopelessly imposing task such as this to see how students react to the challenge, as in: "Are they smart enough to see how broad the issue is and to do something about it?" Will you see the problem? become disillusioned by it? come up with a suitable subtopic?

*Trivial issue or nonissue.* Occasionally, you may be assigned or choose a topic that turns out to be a trivial issue, or not an issue at all. One team, for example, had read a magazine story recently on subliminal advertising and chose this as its issue. It certainly seemed like something that should be an issue. Team members set off to discover the legislative history, interest group positions, policy proposals, and so on. Instead, what they found was one freelance writer who had published a few magazine articles and a book on the subject, along with a small number of academic publications, mostly by marketing professors describing the results of experimental studies with college students. They found no legislative or regulatory action that appeared to be the slightest bit controversial, and thus they had no particular policy problem. After a couple of weeks in disarray, the group went ahead with its topic, setting subliminal advertising into the more general context of deceptive advertising and Federal Trade Commission rules. In doing so, they learned some important lessons in how public issues are generated and public policies formulated, along with the specific knowledge they gained about advertising regulation.

## 2. Policy Background

The second section of your brief expands on the initial description of the issue. It covers the issue's history and current context, the process by which it became an issue, and the chief policy questions it involves.

The difficulties of this section pivot around the demand that a great deal of information be organized and compressed into a few pages. Your task here is an accurate reflection of what professional policy analysts do: compact large amounts of information into a short space while making sure that it makes sense to the audience and is not unfair, oversimplified, or outright distorted.

Clues and insights to the current status of the issue are found in the background analysis. Resist the temptation to skim over this section! Instead, polish it, hone it, write and rewrite it. Your efforts here will establish the foundation for a deeper and sounder policy brief. This component of the report gives the audience a meaty feel for the topic and it clears up anything left unstated in the opening issue-definition section.

## 3. Specific History of the Issue

In this section, concise sketches are drawn of relevant policy actions (media attention, major initiatives, actions by stakeholders, congressional hearings, legislation, lawsuits, incremental or unintended processes, and so on) to illustrate how the specific issue has unfolded.

The emphasis in this section is less on analysis than on a chronology of critical events leading to the present state of the issue. Indeed, it is most useful while research is underway to literally construct a chronology, using note cards that can be spread out on a table, so the team can see the actual sequence of events as they unfolded. This section obviously will draw upon and extend the background portion of the analysis; your audience cannot keep up with volumes of names, dates, and places unless you have developed a context within which to place them.

### 4. Stakeholder/Interest Group Analysis

*Stakeholder* is a term borrowed from management literature. A stakeholder is defined as "any group or organization that can affect or is affected by the achievement of a company's objectives."[2] Although Freeman argues that organizations can have stakeholders but issues cannot, there is a logic that suggests that issues, too, can have their stakes and stakeholders. Freeman's definition can be modified to say that a stakeholder is "any group or organization that can affect or is affected by the outcome of a social or public policy issue."

Once an issue is chosen for study, it is possible to construct an *issue set*, showing how various interest groups or stakeholders become involved in a public issue because it is related somehow to other issues the groups consider important.[3] For example, groups may become involved in the public policy issue of nuclear power plant regulation because of a primary interest in ensuring neighborhood beauty and safety, keeping electric utility rates low, encouraging scientific or military uses of nuclear power, fostering energy conservation, or preventing environmental pollution. Groups with these interests are not so fascinated with nuclear power in its own right, but only because nuclear power is related to an issue they believe in strongly. Another illustration appears in Figure 2.2, which shows also how an issue set can be visually portrayed.

As you can see, to be a stakeholder means to have an interest in the process or outcome of the issue. Some stakeholders may want things to stay the same; some may favor small

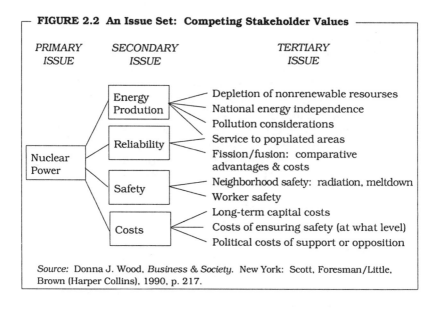

**FIGURE 2.2  An Issue Set:  Competing Stakeholder Values**

| PRIMARY ISSUE | SECONDARY ISSUE | TERTIARY ISSUE |

Nuclear Power

Energy Prodution
- Depletion of nonrenewable resourses
- National energy independence
- Pollution considerations

Reliability
- Service to populated areas
- Fission/fusion:  comparative advantages & costs

Safety
- Neighborhood safety:  radiation, meltdown
- Worker safety

Costs
- Long-term capital costs
- Costs of ensuring safety (at what level)
- Political costs of support or opposition

Source: Donna J. Wood, *Business & Society*. New York: Scott, Foresman/Little, Brown (Harper Collins), 1990, p. 217.

changes of various sorts; some may want radical change. There may be stakeholders who are not involved in any controversy or policy process, yet have an interest in the issue. (For example, this is true of many mental health services consumers.)

Active stakeholders— whether organizations or groups, or occasionally individuals— seek to affect the current policy because of some interest they hold. This does not imply that all stakeholders are involved for purely selfish reasons (some may be altruistic, public spirited, or acting on behalf of others), although it is likely some of them are.

The team's job is to identify the stakeholders, what their interests and positions are, if and how they attempt to influence policy (in the past, present, and future, if it is known) and finally, to the extent possible, how they deal with and relate to one another. Pay special attention to telling the audience who these stakeholders are in a meaningful way; merely listing them will not tie them to the story that is emerging in your issue brief.

Some typical questions to answer about stakeholders are these:

1. Are the stakeholders private or nonprofit interest groups? trade or professional associations? public officials? private citizens?

2. Who are their members? how are they funded? how influential are they? what are their resources?

3. What are their official reasons for taking a position on the issue?

4. Are there unofficial reasons for the position they take? That is, can you discern reasons for their involvement that are not mentioned in their literature or in news stories about them? If so, what is your evidence?

5. What strategies and tactics do they use to achieve their aims?

6. How successful have they been at influencing public policy?

7. Where are they headed with regard to the issue?

A stakeholder map, where all the relevant players (and sometimes their interests) are presented visually, is an excellent way for the team to begin to make sense of things to itself and, most importantly, when the presentation is made, to its audience. A simple stakeholder map is illustrated in Figure 2.3, for the public policy issue of mandatory recycling. A stakeholder map can be used with an overhead projector in your oral presentation. It will become an important visual portion of your written product as well.

**FIGURE 2.3  A Stakeholder Map**

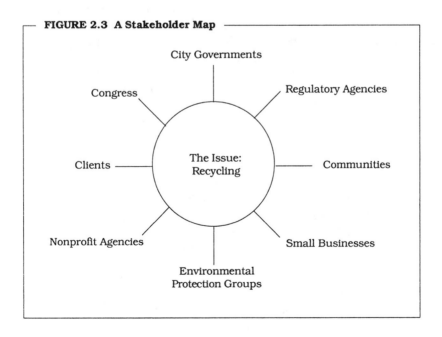

## 5. Disinterested (Society's) Policy Recommendations

After the evidence on all sides— as many sides as there are— has been gathered, the team offers its own policy recommendations (for example, new legislation, regulation, incentive systems, tax reforms, organizational reform, doing nothing), first taking the perspective of an unbiased public policy maker with no personal interests at stake, only those of society. The team must defend its recommendations in light of its previous analysis, and then speculate on the intended and unintended consequences of the proposals.

If you wish, you and your team members may offer majority, concurring, and dissenting opinions, which accommodate legitimate differences among you. This option is a valuable safety valve if the team experiences deep conflicts over recommendations, as sometimes happens.

## 6. Interest-Based Policy Recommendations

Having assumed the optimum point of view of the public policy maker (considering the best outcome for everyone involved or affected), the team is now asked to take the point of view of a major organizational stakeholder in the issue— a business, an industry, a trade association, a hospital, a regulatory agency, a law enforcement agency, an advocacy group— normally an organization directly relevant to the students' chosen profession. The team's analysis should have prepared it to find a defensible posture in the policy debate.

The exercise of developing policy recommendations from two potentially opposing viewpoints— one disinterested and one very interested in the policy outcome— is a way to get team members with biases or strong convictions to consider the alternative sides of an issue. It is easy to be opposed to another point of view, whether or not there's any evidence to support your own position. But it is quite another thing to seriously consider an opposition view from the standpoint of its advocates. You may find that the bulk of the evidence is on the other side, and that you held your first position in ignorance. If nothing else, you can learn how the enemy thinks, what concepts and techniques they use, what points they hold strongly, and where they are likely to falter.

The interest group analysis and team recommendations emphasize analytical and decision-making experiences for students. These components frequently bring out heated and provocative discussions in the group, resulting in clearer thinking, which accordingly makes for a better, stronger paper and presentation.

### 7. Bibliography

Full references of materials used in preparing the brief are required, including such sources as government documents; theoretical and empirical research publications; commentary, debate, features, and news reports in the trade, industry, business, and popular press; television or radio news; and any other resources used— for example, in-person or telephone interviews. The style manual or style sheet recommended by your instructor will give you the appropriate format to use for bibliographic references.

### 8. Appendices

Often you will find that certain documents, maps, charts, data, memoranda, news stories, or other evidence would be useful to include in your brief, but that they would weigh down the brief if inserted into it. If you find this to be true, attach the materials as appendices, and refer to them in the text at the appropriate places. (For example, you could write: "For further documentation of this point, see the corporate memos appearing in Appendix A.")

### Closing Comments on the Public-Policy Issue Brief

These components represent the overall structure of a policy issue brief. The structure may be altered or modified to suit the specific nature of the topic or the intentions of the team or the teacher; it can be altered to suit unique objectives, the time available in the course, and so on. Some issues do not fit the format precisely, perhaps because they are too recent or fast breaking to have a substantial written and documented history (regulation of genetic engineering is one example that has come up in our classes); this makes it imperative that teams know how to locate recent information not yet available in many standard library indexes. Other issues— for example, how proposed changes in U.S. antitrust policy might affect a company— are too unwieldy for the team to do a thorough job on each section of the report. Topics such as this must be redefined, condensed, narrowed. In a public policy analysis, some teams may find that their topic has not invited any visible controversy, but that instead numerous interest groups are competing for their own positive policy proposals. Rather than have the instructor do the redefining for the team, the format incorporates this activity as part of the team's task.

Regardless of the specific nature of the issue, the importance of the format is that it offers a flexible yet systematic way of determining what kind of issue one has and how one should proceed to develop and analyze it. The format is a method of *discovery, analysis, and decision making,* and not merely a static research model where portions are filled in.

## COMPONENTS OF THE STRATEGIC-MANAGEMENT ISSUE BRIEF

The particular focus of a strategic-management analysis can vary significantly from that of a public-policy issue brief. For example, the unit of analysis may be an industry, corporate headquarters, a division or strategic business unit. Yet there are basic components of an analysis that are presented here that give you the flexibility to prioritize components or modify the format as required (see Figure 2.4).* The general components are as follows.

### Issues Definition

A clear statement of the purpose for presenting the case is needed. What is the particular problem, or set of problems, facing this company? Included is a comparative description of the organization's features and introductory remarks that show how it is either unique from or similar to other companies in the industry and/or in society; some companies may be both unique and similar along critical dimensions.

---

* For more useful insights into preparing a strategic-management issue brief, see Power, et al., (1986), *Strategic Management Skills.*

## Industry Context

In which industry or industries does the company operate? What is the company's industry history? (for example, dominance and large market share; former dominance, now in decline; innovator; me-too follower of other companies; low-price or high-quality strategies). How competitive have firms in the industry been over time? What are the main historical features, issues, and challenges of the industry? What are the major forces (technological, political, economic, social/cultural) operating in the industry now and what appear to be the major forces that will affect the industry in the future?

## Current Strategy in Historical Context

This is a summary of the *company's* strategy, with an explanation of the forces and factors that have brought it to its current mission (the company's answer to the query: why do we exist?) and strategies (the plan for achieving the mission). For example, this analysis may include actions taken by past or present company leaders, actions of competitors, changes in the industry brought on by technological inventions or developments, events occurring in the larger society (war, depression, political or demographic changes), responses to governmental actions, and so on. The task here is to provide a context in which to understand and explain the company's current mission and strategy and to lay a basis for understanding opportunities, options, and obstacles for the company in the future.

---

**FIGURE 2.4  Outline for a Strategic-Management Issue Brief**

1. Issues definition
2. Industry context
3. Current strategy in historical context
4. External environmental assessment
5. Internal environmental assessment
6. Strategy evaluation
7. Strategy recommendations
8. Bibliography and appendices

## External Environmental Assessment

This section, which is broader and more detailed than the industry context section, allows you to examine and detail the specific environmental contingencies facing the company. The central aims are to identify and assess, to the extent possible, threats and opportunities that face or could face the firm. A crucial question motivating external environmental assessment is: what does it take to be successful in this business?

It is ironic but true that planning is most likely to be accurate and successful when the environment is stable, although it is most badly needed when the environment is turbulent (rapidly changing). Forecasting is often rooted in assessing past events, and may ignore creative modeling of how events are changing and might change the external environment. Virtually no organization's environment is static and unchanging, and some are so dynamic that they are unpredictable in the short term, much less the long term. The character and state of the external environment, therefore, is a central factor affecting the company's ability to make strategy.

## Internal Environmental Assessment

In this section you will assess the company's internal capabilities, its strengths and weaknesses, in areas such as these: management capabilities, organizational culture, human resources, marketing, financial status, R and D, and operational control systems (including the management information system). Some of this needed information may be sketchy or even inaccessible to your team; do not attempt to cover this up, acknowledge these limitations in your report.

With this information, a company's strategy can be assessed in relation to its strengths and weaknesses. As a result, areas that need improvement or that may be built on are identified and linked to strategy recommendations.

## Strategy Evaluation

Now the team is prepared to make a judgment on the match among the company's strategy, its internal environment, and the external environment. This section addresses the company's objectives in terms of how well they fit with the opportunities and threats in the external environment and the strengths and weaknesses in the company's internal environment. Your team should be prepared to present and defend what you see as correct and incorrect in the firm's strategy.

### Strategy Recommendations

Recommendations flow naturally from the preceding components. The team may choose to make several kinds of recommendations. For example, a team could recommend that current strategy be elaborated and improved; that improvements be made in operational areas so that current strategy can be implemented; or that the company's mission and strategy be drastically overhauled. Whatever the specific recommendations, they must be supported by the evidence presented and the analysis made. Seat-of-the-pants decision making is not the rule in policy analysis.

### Bibliography and Appendices

The same specifications about references and sources cited for the public policy analysis apply to the bibliography of a strategic-management issue brief. Also, additional supporting materials can be included as appendices and mentioned where appropriate in the body of the paper. Appendices, remember, are there for readers who want detail that is unnecessary to the strength of the argument. So don't hesitate to provide them if you think they are helpful, but don't rely on them to justify conclusions or just to take bulk out of the body of the paper.

### *CONCLUSION*

In this chapter we have introduced the public-policy and strategic-management issue brief formats. In the remaining chapters we go into detail on the nuts and bolts of constructing an issue brief and coping with the team that is doing it.

Regardless which of the two formats is used— and analytical areas other than public policy and strategic management can be accommodated by them— the basic processes of topic definition and refinement, research and analysis, supporting recommendations, and methods of presentation are identical. The issue brief formats are adaptable to a wide range of topics and issues because they provide a logical structure for information gathering and decision making.

## ENDNOTES

1. Aaron Wildavsky, *Speaking Truth to Power: The Art and Craft of Policy Analysis* (Boston: Little, Brown), 1979, p. 2.
2. R. Edward Freeman, *Strategic Management: A Stakeholder Approach* (Boston: Ballinger Books (Harper Collins)), 1984.
3. Donna J. Wood, *Strategic Uses of Public Policy* (Boston: Ballinger Books (Harper Collins)), 1986; and Donna J. Wood, *Business and Society* (Glenview, IL: Scott, Foresman/Little Brown (Harper Collins)), 1990.

# 3

## WORKING IN A TEAM

The team processes of preparing either a public-policy or strategic-management analysis are indistinguishable, as both involve the generic steps of team formation, task allocation, research, topic analysis and synthesis, conflict management, and the organization and presentation of written and oral reports.

The generic format for teamwork on each of these types is intended to make the research and analysis task an efficient *team* undertaking, while allowing members to learn about the welter of components that comprise and affect policy and decision making.  By doing team-based research, your team is brought closer to the real world of policy and strategy than it would be through lectures, class discussions, or individual term papers.

In preparing a team-researched brief, you learn a lesson of relevance to your professional lives: that although gathering and analyzing evidence are essential parts of policy making, policies and strategies themselves are made under varying degrees of political bargaining and conflict; incomplete, unclear or absent evidence; conflicting or ambiguous goals and values; and the actions of competing stakeholders who typically have different degrees of power and interest in the policy or strategy.  Indeed, in constructing your paper and presentation, you should see the team as a microcosm of these various forces at work when you evaluate incomplete or ambiguous evidence, disagree over how to analyze and synthesize the issue, bargain or are in conflict over decisions, and so on. What you must do—despite these obstacles, which you will routinely encounter in professional life—is to develop, as a team, a position (and minority positions, as needed) that is defensible, with logical arguments and evidence, on a public-policy issue or a management strategy.

### THE NATURAL HISTORY OF THE ISSUE BRIEF

Regardless of whether the team is examining a public-policy or strategic-management issue, there is a sequence of events, a natural history of sorts, that normally takes place in preparing a written and oral policy brief. Team members can monitor the group's progress in accordance with this sequence.

Each phase of a group project generates its own problems, confusion, or dilemmas for the team members. Many of the decisions and difficulties you will face are perfectly normal, and as you go through this book you will be able to consider whether solutions other teams have designed might work for your particular problems. The sequential phases are given below, with short discussions of problems common to each stage.

**1. Team formation.** This is the critical first phase of the process. Shortly we will discuss how to form a coherent group from a collection of people who, by choice or mandate, find themselves working together.

**2. Topic selection.** Topic selection is handled differently according to the aims of the professor, and consequently poses various challenges and opportunities to the team. For instance, is the topic assigned? May the group select its own topic? May the group alter or redefine the topic? Each situation generates its own opportunities and problems, as we discuss in an upcoming chapter.

**3. Initial research and learning to use resources.** This is yet another point where the project may flounder or blossom.

fogging the glass.

The bone you throw, a place
in history, moves in its
own slow circle, out of reach.
I'd rather lie by the hearth,
belly warm as orange-char embers.
Or wade in spring-swollen rivers
That melt grey cool stones
with slick agility.

Sometimes I dream that I'm
leading a pack through this night sky.
I almost hear them barking + whining,
eager to join me as the earth drops
away.
But then I realize it's my own
hollow panting I hear,
shivering the dead air of this closed compartment,
fogging the glass with its warm breath
as I gnaw my tail + wait.

The creative use of informational resources (human, print, electronic) makes an analysis substantive, up-to-date, and accurate.

A good team realizes that preparing the issue brief isn't the same as writing a term paper, and it cannot possibly be done the night before. To get the job done, you should behave like detectives and track down an issue with nonstandard as well as standard research techniques. As the critical groundwork of finding out what sources are available proceeds, the group naturally moves back and forth from this initial research to preliminary analysis and then into a formal analysis.

**4. *Issue refinement.*** Researching and refining the topic are naturally compatible activities. The team may wish to (or need to) redefine the issue as it sifts through the research findings and collected information. For example, the policy being studied may be complex and have a vast history that makes it unmanageable, or the topic may appear to represent a social problem but not a policy issue. Redefinition may involve broadening, narrowing, or changing the question entirely.

This phase may occur at various stages of the team's work, as it depends on the knowledge that team members bring to the topic assignment or have gathered during the research for it. Such modification of the topic should be done with the instructor's approval or knowledge, to avoid unpleasant surprises. However, it is not the instructor's role to redefine the issue for the team. It is each member's role to evaluate the proposed redefinition and give support and criticism to the team in this frequently difficult procedure.

**5. *Monitoring the research in progress.*** Usually, the hardest work begins for students and the instructor sometime around midterm. Once the preliminary research and analysis have been done, the team members now see the scope of the project, are beginning to wrestle with related issues, and perhaps, to their dismay, are finding few answers or (for some topics), an overwhelming and confusing array of answers. This is *very* common, especially if you are taking the issue seriously!

You typically will find it an anxious period because you are having difficulty locating or understanding information and resources, or in clarifying the issue and sorting out the evidence in terms of relevance, importance, and credibility. This may move your team toward redefining the issue. At this stage, there is potential for high intragroup tensions and trouble with laggard and other difficult members. Finally, there are time constraints and demands beyond the issue brief that the *team* must handle, especially other classes and personal lives (for example, looking for a job as graduation nears).

If your team has developed good trust and a contractual relationship (discussed in Chapter 1), you will eventually navigate through this difficult time and feel the better for it once you get through it. This turmoil and confusion are normal and part of the creative and learning processes in which your team is engaged.

In this strenuous phase, team members are actually sharpening the intellectual, time-management, and group-dynamics skills necessary to finish the project. Despite all these obstacles, if your efforts are sincere, the group will naturally move toward making sense of the research and then will experience the pieces falling into place as you prepare to present your findings and recommendations to the class.

**6. Oral presentation.** If the instructor assigns an oral presentation, ordinarily to be delivered near the end of the term, each team presents its findings and recommendations to the class members according to a set of criteria that may be predetermined by the instructor or developed within the class itself. (We suggest that you follow one of the issue brief formats— public policy or strategic management— that are offered in this book.) Each presentation may be evaluated by the instructor and other class members. Your instructor may decide that a percentage of your final grade will be determined by these class evaluations.

Both presenting and evaluating are often difficult tasks for students. Learning to judge performance, however, is vital to learning about the evaluation of one's professional peers and oneself. Likewise, understanding appropriate techniques of communicating with the audience is crucial to a professional.

**7. The final report.** After a long, hard effort, the written report is ready to be completed and submitted. With so much work already behind you, your team must realize that the permanency of the written word is a critical final factor. We stress that the written report is not a literature review or term paper and that its purpose is to make a concise, critical, summary statement of the policy issue. In most cases it is *not* meant to be, and should not be allowed to be, a lengthy tome. Professional policy analysts know that to be effective they must strive to be concise and precise. Force yourself to learn this style if it does not come easily, for it is a lesson of value in any profession.

Also during this stage, the instructor may decide to have each team member submit an intragroup evaluation of the member's performance and the performance of other group members which, at the instructor's discretion, may count towards the project grade. We recommend that such evaluations be included, since they serve as an incentive for keeping members focused on the task and in a cooperative team spirit.

These are the natural stages that each team, to some extent, passes through as it conducts an analysis of a policy issue. In the next section we'll begin by discussing some issues that affect the process of team formation, and then move to a discussion of team conflict and its resolution.

## ISSUES IN TEAM FORMATION: SELECTING MEMBERS AND GETTING ACQUAINTED

So far we have presented the elements of teamwork without considering the constraints and impediments on a successful team effort or detailing just how the initial formation of the team takes place. You may agree that trust and a contractlike relationship are required, yet be puzzled and ask: "O.K., I still want to know how you get a team started. What are the things to do, the real problems to consider, and how do you deal with them?" It is time to offer a recipe for building a successful team.

As any good cook knows, by faithfully following a recipe (precisely doing certain operations and adding certain ingredients), you do not always get a perfect dish; on-the-spot judgment and reaction are necessary culinary skills. That is, the many variables in cooking make it necessary for good cooks to taste and adapt as they go along. What we say here, then, should be taken with a grain of salt, and as only a general outline that will require on-the-spot adjustment.

A team's strength is that it exists to accomplish a task. There is no uncertainty or ambiguity over why members agree to work together; if they had no common task they would not be a team. It is the primary reason members spend time together and pool their skills, resources, and energy. The focal point of building the team, then, is the commonality of interests and rewards offered by the task, in our case, the policy analysis. No matter what dilemma or difficulty the team encounters in the project, the importance of jointly completing the analysis, which will benefit each member, serves to anchor the team in reality.

Nevertheless, uncertainty and ambiguity is likely to affect a team, especially in its initial phase, as its members grope to join forces and to understand what the analysis requires of them and how to interact with one another. With this in mind, let's consider some common and normal uncertainties and ambiguities facing a team as it forms and begins its work.

### Selecting Members

One important team-building concern is how to select members. For some of our readers the choice is made by a boss, trainer, or professor, who assigns people to work in a group. For those who have a choice in selecting their teammates, there are two considerations. One involves interpersonal dynamics, the other concerns the work-related skills of prospective members.

Thinking about the interpersonal dynamics of a team is difficult and can quickly become confusing as you attempt to anticipate how several people will relate to each other as pairs and then all together as a team. It is better to break down this problem into smaller units, first asking yourself if you get along with prospective members A, B, and C and then, if you do, going on to ask if they get along with each other, and then asking yourself if you *think* you all can get along together.

Even if you decide all potential members get along, you should pause for a moment to reflect on what it means to get along. Does it mean you have a wonderful time gabbing or partying? Or does it mean that you have reason or experience to believe that you can *work* well together, despite any personal likes, attachments, dislikes, or tensions that exist? There is nothing inherently wrong or right about working with close friends or, on the other hand, with people to whom you do not feel close or even dislike. If you feel that getting work done will take second place to a distracting relationship with a person, you are better off not being on a team together or, at the least, you should have a serious talk about whether both of you can be in a team where the emphasis is on work.

Along the same line, you should ask yourself when considering working with close friends if your friendship might be endangered by the demands of teamwork. Can you confront your friends or be confronted by them about your work without being outraged or feeling betrayed? (Bruised feelings and some anger are normal in teamwork.) Would you feel obliged to defend your friends even if they were in the wrong? Are your friendships too delicate or too special for a work-centered relationship? Be serious about this; we have seen the best of friends decide that it is better for them to work separately.

In short, ask yourself about the ways in which you know prospective team members. Can they provide the performance needed in the team? Can your relationships with each of them, good or bad, accommodate the work-first orientation that will be developed in the group?

As you consider the interpersonal dynamics of joining up with certain people, you should also consider the skills they might contribute to the team. The needs of the team vary with the nature of the project and the issue to be researched. You might need to look for members with specialized skills or training, say, knowledge of computer science and information systems or economics; or you might look for generic skills such as the ability to analyze complex problems, to be creative, to write or speak clearly, to conceptualize and produce professional-looking graphics, or to keep the flustered feelings of others under control.

Keep in mind that the nature of the assignments can have a large impact on the skills you seek in team members. Generally, especially if the members do not know one another well, people try to team up with those who appear to be trustworthy, smart, reasonable, hard-working, and knowledgeable of the assignment. It is not unheard of for a person to suddenly become a favorite candidate of several teams because of expertise in the assigned topic. This is tempting for obvious reasons, but be certain the interpersonal dynamics question is not ignored in the rush to recruit the person who knows all about the topic. (And, of course, favorite candidates are not likely to take kindly to those who expect them to do it all.)

Having said this about member selection, a few comments are in order on what we typically observe. Most student teams are composed of people who are acquainted but are not the best of friends. Students frequently select teammates by making an overall, loosely constructed judgment of one another, and by anticipating how it would be to work with those people in a team. Sometimes, however, they do not judge, they merely join a team unthinkingly, a passive choice they may later regret. If you have the opportunity to *select* teammates, do so on whatever criteria you think are most important to a successful project. Don't get stuck in a poorly functioning, hostile, sloppy, or lazy group because you did not make an effort to choose your teammates.

### Getting Acquainted

When people are getting acquainted, there is always a certain amount of uneasiness, tension, posturing, and uncertainty present. Since the team needs to build trust, time spent breaking the ice is a good way to settle down anxious or cautious members and for everyone to feel each other out. If everyone knows one another to some degree, there is no need for members to introduce or formally tell the others about themselves; they just talk with and try to learn more about each other. If, however, each person is not close to or even familiar with more than one or two other members, a round-robin introduction where each one gives a short personal introduction is in order. This can be useful even among students who have been attending the same program, if they have not yet had opportunities to work closely together.

Teams will vary in what members find appropriate to say about themselves. Many students are good at establishing an atmosphere of acceptance, open communication, and support in a group. Those who can comfortably do this will take the lead in making certain that every member speaks and reveals more about themselves than their name and major area of study. Group members will have to sense how much they want to know about one another and where to draw the line in offering information. Someone in the group will need to step in and tactfully call a halt if any members show signs of seeing the team as either too intrusive or, alternatively, as a therapy or rap session.  As a guide to what is appropriate and inappropriate information to offer and to seek from others, think of this as a professional working team.  Ask yourself how a team of professionals would get to know one another, and then do it.

For those who still are wondering how professionals do this, there are several ways to get to know one another.  Many teams naturally get started with a free-for-all bull session at the start of the first meeting.  Another method, a bit more formal, is to intersperse a discussion of yourself, your experiences, interests, or career goals with a preliminary discussion of your ideas on how you connect to the task and the team's division of labor. For example, someone may say: "Well, some day I want to be in charge of a management information system, so I'm very interested in finding out about how Acme Company's MIS was developed and implemented as part of our overall assignment on the company's ability to integrate its strategy and information systems."  If members do not know when to stop talking about themselves, it is easy for a member to politely interrupt by saying: "That's good, John.  It's fortunate that this assignment fits right in with your plans.  Jayne, how about you? Where does the project fit into your plans and interests?"  In this manner it is easy for members to get to know one another, with an occasional shy person needing to be drawn out of a shell and an occasional constant talker (a too-vocal type we cover below) needing to be gently encouraged to let others have a say.  Finally, there is nothing wrong with the classic round-table approach, wherein members offer their names and some other relevant information:  "I'm Susan Smith from Peoria; I'm majoring in political science, and I hope to become a diplomat after graduating from law school."

## TYPES OF TEAM MEMBERS: HANDLING
## THE NORMAL CHALLENGES

There are normal types of team members who pose a challenge, and even an occasional threat, to the operation of the team.  We call them *normal* because they are so often found on teams. Such members are not only a drain on the team, however.  They can make positive contributions, and what we say below should not be taken as a subtle message that a group with any of these normal types is in trouble or will lose its valuable energy because of them.

The normal types include those who are laggards, manipulators, shy or quiet, too vocal, chronic arguers, balkers, seemingly disinterested, and those who want to take charge. Our experience is that the vast majority of teams have at least one of these types, and some teams have several types.

The more troublesome varieties of team members can on occasion pose a threat to the team's success. Such people can slow or ruin the team's efforts, although they usually can be brought on board with a little attention and conscious direction from the team. Remember that as a team forms, it develops rules and psychological commitments in its members that act to bind the team together. This serves to make many potentially troublesome members *want* to contribute to the group. Another way to put it is that as the team takes shape, a group unity arises that channels such members toward shared goals. Let's consider a few examples of normal types.

What about a *seemingly disinterested* member who says at the first meeting: "Man, I don't care how this gets done. I'm graduating in May and I'm out of here." The ultimate need is not to chastise or lecture I-Don't-Care, it is to bring that person into the team.

Of course, it will not do to simply say "join the team" to an I-Don't-Care; that is a paternalistic lecture that few people receive favorably. When teams are forming, I-Don't-Care announcements of disinterestedness are not uncommon. They frequently show signs of anxiety or of a defensive distancing from the group while the members reserve their trust and commitment. Comments like this should never be totally ignored, however, as if they had not been uttered.

A useful tactic is to laugh at it good-naturedly, which releases tension and avoids an embarrassing period of stunned silence. Then follow it up with a comment like: "Yeah, I know John, graduation's been a long time coming. But the end's in sight and we're counting on you to help us do X (whatever John is particularly good at) on this project." Here the member acknowledges the seemingly disinterested member's viewpoint without attacking him and, importantly, without giving legitimacy to his cynical statement.

The team must diffuse I-Don't-Care's reluctance and attach this person's aspirations to the project. Is the member merely tired of school (suffering from "senioritis") and in need of a pep talk about how doing a good job will keep this person's grade point average up? It might be useful to remind I-Don't-Care that the project could help in finding a job, since some employers do want to see samples of applicants' written work, especially that done on a real-world policy analysis. Depending on this person's response, members will get an understanding of how serious, defensive, or feigned the disinterest is. Often it is nothing more than a way to draw attention and to get reassurance that the others really do care about doing a good job. A seemingly disinterested person may have other pressing concerns and an understanding approach by the team usually works to open up this type of member enough to admit an obligation to the team, despite whatever else may be troubling or demanding time.

A single member's disinterestedness, which indicates an unwillingness to commit to the team, is likely to give way to team membership and participation. It is difficult for one person to be in a group where the member is implicitly communicating to the others: "I'm special and do not want to work as hard as you do. I know you will accept my standards even though they are very low and may hurt your grade and what the professor and our fellow students think of you."

If, over several meetings, none of the team's efforts make a difference with I-Don't-Care, then it is time to directly confront this person and ask on what terms, if any, I-Don't-Care is willing to be a fully contributing team member. Teams rarely have a member who simply refuses to participate, since that would translate directly into nonmembership, although we have seen this happen. More often, the seemingly disinterested member avoids confrontation with defenses such as: "Sure, anything you say," or, "That's O.K. with me." To make sure the member means what is said, you need only to assign some work and then see if and how it gets done. As the last resort, a disinterested member may be (1) asked to leave the group ; (2) told that a low rating on the team's internal evaluation will be forthcoming; or (3) asked by the team to consult with the instructor.

The situation is more dangerous if there is more than one I-Don't-Care on a team. The potential for a coalition where each psychologically supports the other exists, and that is more likely to pose a serious problem than one disinterested member. The main difference between one and two or more disinterested members lies in the isolation/support dimension. One disinterested member is easily isolated by receiving no team support and feels strong discouragement for the disinterested behavior. Two or more I-Don't-Cares, however, form a subgroup that offers psychological support and justification to resist the others, (for example: "These dummies think we're going to do what they want! Well, we've got more important things to do, don't we!").

This double I-Don't-Care situation rarely arises, but if it does, the team should not fool itself into thinking that the disinterested members will come around in the end. Chances are that they will not, and that one or two or three members will do most of the work, while the others take a free ride. In an infrequent instance such as this, the alternatives available are to: (1) try to break up the subgroup by encouraging, assigning, or enticing its members into different task-related subteams; (2) separate into two groups (although this may not be possible for a number of reasons); (3) have an airing-out, conflict-resolution session, discussed later in the chapter, to see if there is any solution acceptable to the entire group; (4) seek the intervention of the professor (a last resort measure); and finally (5) threaten the subgroup with the consequences of poor internal team evaluations, a procedure where each member rates the others on their contributions to the group. (More will be said on internal evaluations later in the book. Here we note that members who do not contribute their share may receive a low or failing grade in the project if other members report and *document* poor or no performance.)

Occasionally, teams will have a member who steadfastly acts like a curmudgeon or *chronic arguer.* The benign form of the chronic arguer is one who argues for the love of it and then does every task that is required, merrily grumbling all the way. Frequently, these people are valuable team members because they sharpen team analysis and reasoning by making challenges that could come from an audience or critical commentators. Often, a chronic arguer of this sort responds well to direct feedback, even if the feedback is only: "That's a stupid idea" or, "We don't want to talk about that now." Members will have to judge how to deal with such persons by keeping in mind that not all members are going to be cooperative all the time. And it is important to remember that the arguer's points may be worth hearing, and not chalk up this type of member as a useless windbag.

There is a fine line between the more or less harmless chronic arguer and a person who genuinely will *not*, for whatever reason, reach an agreement with other people. The format given for the policy analysis requires that the team take the view of an interested party (a stakeholder or actor) and allows for those with dissenting views to file a minority report with their alternative analysis of the topic. In this way, if it becomes necessary, a chronic arguer can make a contribution of research and analysis for the entire project, and be reassured by the right to file a minority report. Chronic arguers are allowed to present viewpoints in an intellectual context and cannot claim, as this type might, that the group has acted as a tyrant or that their insights will never be on the record or be given a fair hearing by the audience. In other words, the option to present a minority report can be used to call the bluff of a chronic arguer. In a similar and less dramatic fashion, the issue brief format calls for the team to consider alternative points of view as part of its task. This has obvious benefits for dealing with chronic arguers whose argumentativeness can be channeled into raising alternative viewpoints.

The *take charge types* need to be maneuvered into recognizing, or at least observing, the rights, responsibilities, and views of others. Some people are so full of self-confidence or are so self-centered that they honestly believe themselves experts on everything and see themselves as the obvious and only leaders in all circumstances. As with the other types, a take-charger can be neutralized or used to advantage by the team through the rules it develops. For example, with a person bent on taking control who indicates, either in action or in words, to the team: "I can handle this, just sit back and let me take charge," it may be necessary to establish an explicit rule for consensus decision making. This would allow members to tell the take-charger that they appreciate this person's energy and guidance, yet they want to share in all decisions because the team will function better that way, they will learn more about working in a group that way, or they want the experience of making consensual decisions as professional peers. Few take-charge types can mount an effective argument against team democracy, but it is necessary that the team stick to it decision, since take-chargers usually try to get control more than once and if blocked, can be quite clever about it.

*Quiet types* are unknown quantities to team members. (Is she smart, dull, disinterested, passive-aggressive, creative but withdrawn, tired, worried, bored? Does he think he's better than the rest of us? Why won't she participate? Are we going to have to carry him for this whole project?) Without information sharing and feedback from quiet members, the rest of the team will not know how to arrange properly the mutual burdens and benefits of teamwork.

If a special effort is needed to draw a quiet type into team discussions, make it. But be careful not to do it in a fashion that makes the quiet one feel patronized or on display. Try not to assume what the quiet type is like or capable of unless you have solid evidence; in a team effort you want to find out what the quiet types' interests, skills and capabilities are and how they can benefit the team—you do not want to write off members on the basis of a first impression.

We have seen vastly differing quiet types, and so have you, if you think about it. Some are quiet by nature, some because of a recent event (serious illness or accident, death in the family, low score on an entrance exam). Some are slow learners, some are phenomenally bright and gifted, and others are keen observers who would rather watch than participate in group activities. Get them talking and show them that they can feel comfortable with the team. Above all, do not ignore or demean them with such actions as giving them the dirty work no one else wants to do. This isolates and alienates them and allows them to withhold their potential from the team, and it is unfair to them.

The type who poses the most potential harm for the team is the *manipulator*. To manipulate means to manage or influence in an unfair manner. Therefore, the manipulator is a direct threat to the team's trust. Some members manipulate to get out of doing work and some do so out of a psychological desire to create conflict or rivalries in the team.

Those who try to manipulate to avoid work are controllable through team rules, as long as the members do not make exception after exception, to the point that the rules no longer are enforced. For example, if a member does not do the assigned work on time and has an excuse the team accepts, this member should be informed, gently yet firmly, that given the short time in which the analysis must be done, the work must be made up soon. Then, the manipulator can commit to doing the work on a timetable, or for the next meeting, or whatever it takes to make it clear that the work is important and that the manipulator, not others, has the responsibility to get it done. It is not always easy to deal with manipulators, as they are skilled at exploiting the generous and supportive sentiments in others.

Many of the manipulators we have seen or been informed of are skillful at getting others to feel sorry for them and to help them by doing their work or covering for them. This is particularly difficult if the manipulator is your friend. A graphic example of this occurred in a team one of us had in a class. This team had five members, four of whom were full-time students and one who was an older student working full time. As a consequence, their meetings were few and they had to accomplish a great deal in them. Four of the members worked hard, especially the one with a full-time job, and one of them spent the entire semester making a series of excuses about why his work was not done. The group was tolerant of him largely because (and this is common in groups with manipulators) they did not want to confront him or tell on him. He, of course, knew this, and used the knowledge to his advantage. To add to the matter, his best friend— who was intelligent and hard working— was in the group and took pains to cover for him and to explain away his failure to do any work. Most interestingly, at the end of the semester, just prior to their oral presentation in class, members came to the professor independently to voice concern over his continual failure to work; even his friend reluctantly came in to report on this manipulator's dismal performance.

The professor told each of them that learning to act professionally could involve unpleasant situations where a colleague had to be negatively evaluated. It was explained to each of them that they were not to blame— each showed some guilt over telling on him— for giving an honest evaluation of their peer. Without a poor evaluation in writing, however, the professor would not do anything about this student. Each of them did give him a poor evaluation, citing his missed meetings, leaving meetings early, and failure to do research and to participate wholeheartedly in the analysis and organization of the issue brief. As a result, his grade in the course suffered a drop of one and one half letter grades. The manipulator, of course, was shocked and angered, because he had believed that the rules of the game offered him an easy grade. But the professor had secured enough evidence to justify the penalty, and it stuck.

An impartial, consistent, tough approach to the rules of the team, applied when signs of manipulation are clear, will force the manipulator into action: first, to try new devious tactics and, failing these, either to work or to leave the team. Such application of the rules can help to prevent the situation where team members try to punish the manipulator at the end of the term; not all professors will accept this sort of action, and the group may be stuck with carrying a badly behaving member who has contributed nothing to the project but who earns the same grade as everyone else.

The manipulator who seeks to stir up discord in the team out of some psychological need is a very difficult problem and, fortunately, a very rare type. If a team encounters this problem, it may be dealing with a person who has personality conflicts that should *not* be taken on by the team or any of its members *as a part of the team's responsibility*. In a team project with a small number of people, there is a great amount of work to be done in a short period of time. This mandate should suffice, if it is called upon often enough by team members, to negate most attempts by members to make trouble for trouble's sake. In other words, as some of the teams who have had this problem with manipulators told us: "We were too busy to worry about that stuff, and it was easy to see who was and was not pulling their share of the load." If handled correctly, manipulators may be embarrassed or tacitly coerced into making their contributions.

*Laggards* are those who, for one reason or another, do not get their work done on time. They are not always lazy— they may be slow, procrastinators, inefficient or poorly organized, or truly overworked and unable to accomplish tasks on time. It is important to distinguish these reasons. Those who perform lazily do not identify with the team. Lazy members need prodding and reminding that their contribution is needed on a timely basis. Those who are slow workers may feel thoroughly a part of the team, yet not be able to work up to the standards and time pressures of other members. (If you're a fan of "Mr. Rogers' Neighborhood," you surely know the song that Mr. Rogers sings:

"I like to take my time and do it right." This approach drives the type-A personality crazy, but can be just as productive in the long run as rushing around.)

Slow members may simply need to put in more time than the more efficient members. Those who are inefficient or poorly organized can be encouraged to work smarter, not faster. Sharing time- and paper-management techniques, encouraging the setting and meeting of deadlines, and helping these members set priorities can make a difference in how well and rapidly the project is accomplished. As a side benefit, these members may learn tactics that help them in other areas of their lives as well. Those who are overworked, similarly, may need assistance finding additional resources or in setting priorities.

This business of laggards raises an equity issue, since some members may be tempted to slow down or to remain slow paced once the team labels them as such, while on the other hand, fast-paced and efficient members may feel that too much of the workload falls to them because they know how to get large amounts of work done. If this becomes an issue, the group must resolve it before too much behind-the-scenes grumbling goes on and erodes the team's trust and productivity. Trust is not a static element that is attained once and for all and then never considered again. Trust is the basis from which laggards should be discussed and dealt with.

*Foreign students* are regularly enrolled in many professional schools in American universities. Their presence in a team may require certain courtesies and allowances, as the fact that they are from another culture should not be overlooked. Foreign students may be seen as possessing unique resources that can be of great benefit to the team, and they may be viewed as lacking some insider information and orientation that only a member of the host American culture can provide.

For example, many of the Asian students we have taught are very bright with excellent skills in mathematics and some difficulties expressing themselves in written English. They benefit from practice in writing and special attention (often through private tutoring) to their written language skills. We ask teams who have such members to encourage them to undertake writing assignments and to obtain whatever tutoring or editorial assistance they need. As another example, we have taught students who have extensive experience in international management, as many U.S. business students have not.  Such students have a great deal of knowledge and skill to offer teams.  As still another example, many European and African students are quite fluent in English and have no difficulty expressing themselves, but they do have some differences in the way they perceive group relationships, tasks, behavioral norms, and other culture-specific concepts and phenomena.  Facility with English may encourage U.S. students to perceive such international students as being just like them, when in fact they are not and are operating under different cultural assumptions.

Normally, it is important that no team is composed mostly or entirely of foreign students.  They need to learn about their host culture, and working in a multicultural team is an excellent way to do this.  Equal benefits are available to domestic team members, who learn from their foreign colleagues about how things are done in their countries and who also learn, in the process, how to adapt their own behavior to accommodate and benefit from teammates from other countries.

*In general,* considering the task-oriented status of teams, most members usually want to get the work done.  Those who have reasons or personality characteristics that inhibit a work-first orientation can be controlled by the group's dynamics and by its contractual relationship: focusing on the task, dividing the labor, and adopting rules to work by.  Most issues and problems generated by these normal types can be overcome by the overriding legitimacy of the team's focus on the task.  It is not the type of person per se who creates serious difficulties for the team, but the actions of the team in response to that person which dictates how any potentially troublesome type will affect the team.

## *RELATING COMMUNICATION AND CONFLICT RESOLUTION*

Like leadership, communication and conflict are catchall concepts that are often sloppily employed to explain the achievements or deficiencies of a group.  Communication is frequently viewed, especially by younger students we have observed working in teams, as if it means harmony, honesty, shared understanding, and a lack of conflict.  A lack of communication (usually termed poor communication), then, connotes the opposite.  The relationship between communication and conflict, however, is not this simple.

Communication denotes the transmission of information between persons.  Thinking of communication as harmony and the absence of conflict can lead to confusion and misunderstanding of team processes and dynamics, and to a failure to appreciate and make use of the positive contributions of conflict. Conflict is struggle, strife, disagreement, opposition, argument; it is sometimes dependent on or brought about by *good* (that is, clear, understandable) communication, not by its absence. Let's consider Figure 3.1 to illustrate the possible relationships between conflict and communication.

The most common view of the connection between conflict and communication we encounter among students is found in Cell 2, where conflict is high and communication is poor. That is, students generally believe that conflict and poor communication normally go together. The complementary connotation is that good communication reduces or abates conflict (Cell 3). Sometimes this is correct, but it is not *always* correct.  Consider

**FIGURE 3.1  The Relationship of Communication and Conflict Regarding the Task**

|  | COMMUNICATION | |
| --- | --- | --- |
| *CONFLICT* | *GOOD* | *POOR* |
| High | (1)<br><br>Substantive disagreement; values at stake; clear understanding of positions<br><br>*Negotiation needed.* | (2)<br><br>Disagreement lacking clarity; are values at stake? Understanding is lacking.<br><br>*Values clarification needed.* (Depending on the outcome, go to Cell 1 or 3.) |
| Low | (3)<br><br>Shared agreement on values and substance.<br><br>*Ready to work.* | (4)<br><br>Dininterested members; "Who cares" attitude prevails. False consensus.<br><br>*Team must get to work.* |

that in Cell 2, the failure or inability of teammates to communicate their values regarding the task to one another has led to misunderstandings and conflict. It is possible that conflict is generated by misunderstanding (or miscommunicating, if you like) others' positions and views. If the various positions held in the team can be clarified, members may see that they are in agreement, not disagreement. There is a need to articulate and explore your values regarding the project to see if indeed you really do have a basis for agreement. It is our experience that much of the conflict over group projects falls into this cell.

The relationship pointed out in Cell 1 (high conflict, good communication) is the one students often have a difficult time accepting because it seems counterintuitive that conflict could exist where communication is good. In this scenario, the disagreement in the team is over substantive issues, that is, members understand (or have good communication with) each other very well, but they do not accept one another's views. Teams in this situation do not need *values clarification*, they need to *negotiate* their differences to an acceptable resolution. The difference is substantial in that values clarification implies that if clarification takes place, differences are attenuated or disappear; whereas in negotiation, ways of accommodating genuinely different value positions are sought. (This is not to suggest that value conflict rules out shifts in positions or compromise; quite the contrary. Knowing you have such differences allows you to decide how important they are and how to negotiate a compromise so that the task will get done.)

Teams will face different conflicts over how to do the work for a policy analysis; some will have conflict over how to organize it and draw conclusions; and some teams will have conflict over how much and what kind of work each member does. These are value conflicts, respectively, over working on the project versus other uses of time, how to do the analysis and reach conclusions, and the status of each member in the group.

In Cell 4 we note that the absence of conflict is not in itself a reason to think that all is well with the team. Ironically, it may signify that little or no thought has been given to the task, so that conflict is absent for the wrong reason: no critical work has taken place.

Cell 3 is virtually self-explanatory. It is a setting in which views are shared and agreement is reached so that the work can be done. There is one noteworthy comment in order for Cell 3, and it is that any agreement is dynamic and subject to change, which may in turn create conflict farther into the project. That is, you may agree on what to do now, yet differ on what to do when the next matter comes up. This is perfectly normal and is frequently a sign that the team is intellectually engaged in the project.

## CONFLICT SITUATIONS

As Figure 3.1 illustrates, the existence of conflict in a team is not in itself important. Conflict, under the right circumstances, may be precisely what the team needs to make progress. Alternatively, conflict may indicate that a stalemate is present, as when one member absolutely refuses to accept the positions of other team members and also refuses to negotiate or compromise. Conflict itself is neither good nor bad, positive nor negative, integrative nor disruptive; the substantive reasons for conflict and the results of it are what matter. This is an essential premise for teams to accept if they are to do their best on the project and manage the behavioral dynamics of teamwork. A good team allows and controls conflict; that is, it manages conflict for the improvement of the project.

When conflict in a team occurs, there are three generic solutions that may be reached, but only one of them is recommended by us; the other two (force a solution; dissolve the team) are unsatisfactory resolutions and in almost all instances are avoidable by team members. The optimal solution for team conflict is some form of *negotiated compromise*, where all parties reach a working agreement in which no one wholly disregards or concedes an original position without appropriate cause. A good rule of thumb for negotiating a compromise is that it is unacceptable to compromise your basic ethical and moral convictions— unless you have consciously decided to revise them.

On other matters, such as analytic techniques or research styles, you can take an experimental view. For instance, you might think that other members want to give far too much time to searching for initial information. In such a case, the team might agree that if initial research efforts turn up nothing, and there is reason to think the needed information does not exist, then the team will choose a new topic. On the other side of the issue, those you disagree with may reason that this is a fair compromise as long as you are prepared to go forth with the effort if it looks promising, if you are getting close to something. (This is an example of a compromise on a substantive issue where legitimate concerns about time and the usefulness of evidence are involved. We will comment on *personality conflicts* shortly.)

One of the unsatisfactory solutions to conflict is that one party wins or dominates and the other party loses or becomes subordinate. Win/lose situations are rarely due to one side's superior logic, argument, and overall case; win/lose situations typically occur because one side has a superiority in some vital resource (for example, knowledge of the topic, influence with other team members, a close relationship with the professor, an indefatigable ability to argue [stubbornness], and so on) that allows them to win. Winning and losing have high costs in a team. Losers regularly feel humiliated and less a part of the group, with obvious consequences for their participation in the team. Losers working with winners is akin to barley working with the millstone. And winning is not all it's thought to be; once achieved the winner may feel guilty rather than gleeful, angry rather than satisfied. Even if you know that the other side is wrong, your job as a team member is not to defeat them, but to provide evidence and argument to allow them to modify their position.

A second usually unacceptable solution is for the members in conflict to agree that they cannot reach a compromise and to have the team split up. This should *only* be done after all other options have been explored; we have seen a team do this only once in ten years. Professionals should find some common ground from which they can work together; in fact, a major learning process is for team members to reach resolutions in circumstances of conflict.

In this way, conflict is the springboard to creativity. If you cannot settle a conflict over a substantive issue, in all likelihood you have not been creative enough. Once again, we remind you that the policy research format allows many potential conflicts to be resolved easily by allowing for minority views on the topic to be incorporated into the policy brief, thus accommodating many team conflicts of values or interpretations.

### *CONFLICT RESOLUTION TECHNIQUES*

How do you control conflict? What rules apply? How do you know the difference between destructive and productive conflict? Are there times when conflict should be discouraged? encouraged? How do you deal with personality conflict?

The dynamics of a small team operating within a democratic framework tend to make conflict resolution successful in all but a few instances. This is true because of the trust, fairness, and sense of control shared by the members. Any differences they have, it follows, can be addressed seriously and resolved to everyone's satisfaction. Here are some guideline questions for resolving conflict; they are paraphrased from a review of conflict management done by Thomas.[1]

1. What do the parties feel they have to lose and gain? What is at stake for each party?
2. Definition of the conflict (Which cell in Figure 3.1 are you in?)
   (a) Do you understand one another's position?
   (b) Does the definition of the issue get at the underlying disagreement, or is it a superficial substitute, perhaps for a personality conflict or for a deeper value conflict you do not want to face?
   (c) Can you come up with an alternative definition that settles the conflict?
3. Style of conflict resolution interaction:
   (a) Typically, successful styles are collaborative, sharing, and accommodative, that is, based on trust. (This does not mean you are politely dishonest, submissive, or that you avoid emotional reactions.)
   (b) Unsuccessful styles, especially in the long term, are confrontational, competitive, or avoiding. They are based in mistrust and thinking of oneself at the expense of the team mission.
4. Behavioral dynamics:
   (a) Parties should be aware that they partly influence one another's behavior, that is, if you imply distrust in your behavior or are sarcastic, expect the same in return.
   (b) Are there patterns in how you deal with one another that produce escalation of the conflict?
   (c) Do the parties have a genuine good faith agreement to seek a resolution to the conflict?
5. Are third parties, other team members, or neutral outsiders, available to mediate serious conflicts?

Getting these questions asked and answered may take no more than an hour, or it may require a marathon meeting or perhaps several consecutive meetings. Once such a discussion has occurred, team members will have a good idea of what the conflict is about and how difficult it is likely to be to resolve. Now, here are some specific strategies that can be used to manage conflict:

1. *Provide direct feedback to an angry team member.* As the teammate yells in frustration, say: "You are certainly angry. Your face is getting red. You are shaking your finger in my face." Your lack of response to the content of what is being said, coupled with your immediate and objective response to the inappropriate behavior may take the angry person by surprise and cause this member to calm down and present views more rationally and civilly.

2. *Enlist all team members in conflict resolution.* This strategy is consistent with the democratic decision-making approach to teams, and can be especially effective when conflicts center on facts, interpretations, and knowledge, rather than values or strongly held beliefs.

3. *Arrange a private meeting among conflicting team members and a mediator, preferably an outsider.* Without the pressure of having to perform publicly in the team, the conflicting members may be able to reach a compromise or at least a working agreement.

4. *Elicit the issues involved, write them down, and hold a general team discussion of them.* Using a flip chart or blackboard to write down issues in conflict is helpful because people in disagreement tend to repeat themselves. Once a point is already on the board, however, everyone can see that it's there, and members can be discouraged from returning over and over to the same point without further evidence or logical support.

Conflict resolution in a team is an extension of the team's contractual relationship; conflicts are inevitable, and they must be dealt with if the project is to be accomplished. Those teams that have developed trust will *use* conflict to make a better project.

## PERSONALITY CONFLICTS

What about personality conflict? Often this is a catchall label for any sort of group conflict that people don't want to bother with explaining, much less resolving. After all, it is not really ideas or viewpoints that come into conflict, it is people; and when people argue they frequently raise their voices, seeing others as stubborn or lacking common sense. Given this, it is easy to conclude that they don't like working together because they have a personality conflict. This explanation appears to absolve the group of any responsibility for managing the situation.

Accepting personality conflict as an explanation leaves little room for a successful resolution because it implies that personalities are stable and will not change. When dealing with conflict, do not be hasty in labeling it personality conflict; think of how you can keep the disagreement focused on the project. Even if two members truly do not like each other or bristle at the behavior or manner of one another, you still have room to make accommodations that get the project done. Lastly, in a professional work group, people who do not get along, in varying degrees, frequently work together. If you are genuinely irritated or offended by the style of another member, it is often best to clear the air on it at a group meeting. Do not let it fester because at moments of high stress and anxiety, which are virtually ever-present in this task, an explosion, or an attack of charges and countercharges is probable.

## CONSULTING THE INSTRUCTOR

Many students see the instructor's role as that of a police officer or, even worse, a prison warden. In reality, the instructor is more like a referee and an information booth; most instructors would be delighted to know how teams are doing and to offer suggestions for difficult portions of the project. On the other hand, instructors do not want to hand hold with teams, especially students who aspire to become critically thinking professionals.

As with most things in life, then, there is a balance to strike between knowing when and when not to seek the instructor's advice. For some students, merely being reminded of this balance is sufficient to allow them to judge when they need commentary from the instructor. Nonetheless, here are some things to take into account when deciding whether or not to involve the instructor in your conflict resolution and problem solving.

Whatever the conflict or problem, the cardinal consideration is this: has your team tried seriously to deal with it before taking it to the instructor? An important emphasis of the issue brief project is for students to learn about group dynamics and analytic problem solving experientially and largely on their own, with recourse to the instructor when things are muddled or dire enough to justify it. In other words, you are not abandoned by the instructor, but part of the instructor's aim is to let you learn from solving the problems that routinely arise in team policy analysis, both from group dynamics and the intellectual task. Therefore, before going to the instructor with a conflict problem, ask yourself: "Has the team really tried to work through to a solution?" If not, do so. If so, be prepared to tell the instructor *how* you have tried to cope with the problem. Furthermore, without trying to cast guilt about or accuse or belittle your teammates, you should be prepared to articulate each side of the conflict for the instructor. You may be closer to a solution than you imagine and may realize this in preparing your thoughts to talk with the instructor.

## *CONCLUSION*

The ability to work in teams on policy-analysis tasks is a valuable skill for professionals. Considering the increasing interdependence of modern life, problem-focused teams are regular features in organizations, as they offer significant advantages over what one person can accomplish. In this chapter we covered an introduction to team-based policy analysis and delved into the critical aspects of how teams get started, how they develop a sense of trust that allows them to work in a contractlike relationship, how they might deal with normal types of potentially difficult members, and finally, how they can respect and resolve conflict. You now have the preliminary skills needed to switch your attention back to the team's formal task, and to start dealing with the topic of your research.

## *ENDNOTES*

1. Kenneth Thomas, "Conflict and Conflict Management." In Marvin
   D. Dunnette, Ed., *Handbook of Industrial and Organizational
   Psychology* (Chicago: Rand McNally), 1976, pp. 889–935.

# 4

# DEALING WITH THE TOPIC

Now we go into the nitty-gritty issues of doing a policy issue brief, starting, obviously enough, with the topic itself. Choosing a topic in the first place— if one is not assigned a topic by the instructor— is a matter of combining three factors: (1) the interests of team members, (2) the focus and content of the class, and (3) the availability of resource materials. Once chosen, your topic will need continuing attention. It will tug you in this direction or that, or maybe half a dozen directions at one time; it will throw up roadblocks to the research or open unexpected opportunities; and, if it is a well-chosen topic, it will irritate you, surprise you, and encourage you to learn new skills.

In dealing with the topic, the team faces several concerns: (1) how to decide about broadening, narrowing, switching, radically redefining, or even abandoning the topic, (2) how to do preliminary literature searches to aid in refining and making progress on the topic, and (3) how the group processes of leadership, team building, and task allocation operate in dealing with the topic.

## *REDEFINING THE TOPIC: BROADENING, NARROWING, SWITCHING*

Virtually any topic will need some alteration, from slight narrowing or broadening, to actually reconstructing the question, to switching topics entirely (on rare occasions). You may ask why an instructor would assign a topic that needed modifying, and you may be hesitant to alter the topic because you think that an assigned topic is automatically precise and not subject to redefinition. The instructor, however, may have assigned a topic, fully knowing that the team must redefine it as a necessary part of engaging in a real-life policy analysis. The team should not feel constrained by the original statement of the problem *unless* the instructor gives explicit instructions that the topic must be addressed precisely as assigned.

As your team gets deeper into research and analysis, you will see that you are not always able to tell whether you are sticking with the topic or redefining it. In your more difficult times it is much like dreaming that you are searching for an object that magically disappears or takes on another shape just as you think you have grasped it at last. A good technique for dealing with an ephemeral topic, as most topics are at the beginning, is to keep notes on *how* the team defines the issue as the research and discussions proceed (it is good to end each meeting with a short oral and written summary of how you see the topic). In this way you can see how *what you are learning* about the topic is affecting *how you think* about it. Any decisions about redefining the topic should be made in light of what you have learned from your research.

In most cases, you and your teammates will not recognize that your topic is too narrow, too broad, or improperly defined until the preliminary research has begun. This point bears mentioning because some teams are tempted to redefine the topic without first investigating it (often because it appears overwhelming). Or, in contrast, a team may remain rigidly bound to the original topic statement no matter what they learn from their research. A rule of thumb is that marginal broadening and narrowing are common and that radical redefinition and switching do occur, though more infrequently. That is, the original statement of the problem almost always changes slightly but usually not greatly as you learn more about it. Now for some examples.

### Broadening the Topic

As a case of the need to broaden, consider this topic: *should stricter standards be promulgated and enforced for water pollution control in City X?* Your preliminary research may show that by only considering City *X*, you either do not have enough information to work with or that the issue is better understood in relation to the state and national levels of regulation. You may see from your research that water pollution is one element in a broader environmental context which logically also includes air and noise pollution. As a result of preliminary research, you may decide to broaden the topic to read as follows: *should stricter state and federal standards be promulgated and enforced for water, air, and noise pollution in City X?* This definition permits you to retain the local focus, if that is desirable, but gives you a broader range of environmental concerns so you will actually have something of substance to write about. Or, if you choose to focus on the issue of water pollution alone but can expand the geographic scope of your research, the following broader topic might emerge: *should stricter state (or federal) standards be promulgated and enforced for water pollution in urban areas?* Now, presumably, you have a topic on which there will be sufficient information, one for which you can really produce results.

### Narrowing the Topic

Here's an example of a topic that desperately needs to be narrowed: *what are the benefits and costs of government regulation?* A preliminary search will show you that this is not one topic but many; just consider how widely government regulation is found throughout modern society and the enormous amount of research, debate, legislation, and related information available on it. In the U.S., for example, the subject matter of regulation includes topics as diverse as workplace safety, consumer protection, truth in advertising, the content and labeling of beverages and foods, testing and distribution of pharmaceuticals, shipping routes, quantities of various exports and imports, and a great deal more.

The preliminary search will give you a quick overview of the scope of your too big topic, thus suggesting smaller topics that might be appropriate for research. From initial research, a team would quickly see that the government's regulatory role is so vast and complex that the only way to handle the issue is to narrow it down to a manageable problem such as this: *what are the costs and benefits of government regulation of corporate mergers?* Or perhaps: *what are the costs and benefits of government regulation of pharmaceutical innovation?* Even these are formidable topics, but they are more feasible and can be refined progressively as the preliminary research is done.

**Switching The Topics**

When research on the topic gets rolling, teams are likely to develop a clearer sense of the complexities and demands of the topic, and in this way members become competent to narrow or broaden it as needed. The conditions for switching to another topic are more clear-cut and less commonly encountered.

The primary criterion for switching topics is that *little or no information from any source is available on the issue*, as when you have a topic such as: *how has ball-bearing production in Country X contributed to the trade deficit in the United States?* A team will have to do a considerable amount of searching before reaching the conclusion that not enough data exists, however, since many times in policy research it is not that little exists on the topic, but that the team is not looking in the right places.

Some policy issues are so new that little or no legislation or documentary evidence or research on them exists; this situation, for instance, characterized the genetic engineering issue in the early 1980s. Other policy issues have not been addressed in a policy context, so that little policy-related information on them exists. One team found this to be true of their chosen issue of subliminal advertising, and they switched topics because of the lack of policy-related information. In cases such as these, you have grounds for switching topics once you have documented that there is not enough information available to address the issue.

But let's pause a moment. Remember that a lack of directly pertinent printed materials need not necessarily be a reason for switching topics. It may be an opportunity to be creative by interviewing those working in the area, getting yourself up-to-date on pending legislation or stakeholders' strategies as events are taking place, locating and analyzing relevant data that bear on the issue, and then devising a scenario about how the policy arena of this topic will unfold from society's point of view and also from that of a stakeholder.

It is easy to conclude that very new topics do not have a historical context, but if you make the effort to search, you will almost always find the historical roots of an issue. Never mind that they have been overlooked until recently, they are there. The trick is to discover where to locate these historical roots. In such an instance, your team would ferret out and connect seemingly disparate evidence on the current policy topic, and this could be a main contribution of your analysis.

In sum, switch topics as a last resort, but first consider how you can turn the disadvantage of little available documentary evidence into an opportunity to be creative and make a contribution to understanding.

### Radically Redefining the Topic

The criterion for radical redefinition of the problem is that the problem as stated does not adequately address or misconstrues the assigned policy issue. For example, one student we know was required to analyze a real-world policy issue and was given the following assignment: *evaluate conflicting claims over no-fault and tort-based automobile insurance rate plans in the state of Pennsylvania. Which, if any, of these claims is correct?*

The student, after reviewing the evidence, decided that the claims could not be evaluated accurately because the data available were the product of a fundamental conceptual confusion in existing state automobile insurance laws. That is, the central and unstated premise of the research question was that the state had tried both the no-fault and tort systems. In fact, however, the state's so-called no-fault law had mixed aspects of both tort and no-fault conceptions of liability. Therefore, there were no data available to answer the question of which system was best at holding down automobile insurance rates. This insight led the student to redefine the question from an evaluation of existing data (which were judged to reflect the problem, not to answer it) to a consideration of the concepts of no-fault and tort-based insurance legislation themselves. In summary, instead of evaluating existing data to settle a policy question, as the topic assignment implied, the student redefined the question after reviewing the evidence and thinking through the policy-reflected logic of two liability systems (while staying within the overall bounds of the topic). The final topic was a consideration of the consequences (in terms of insurance rates) of the legal concepts underlying the state's insurance laws.

**Know What the Instructor Expects**

How do you know when a topic is too big and needs to be narrowed, or too small and needs to be broadened? With some issues, such as examining nationwide or global policy issues, the scope is obviously too broad, but with many issues, your team may be fuzzy about whether you are attempting too much or too little.

Ultimately and pragmatically, the answer is tied to the instructor's intentions about the scope of your project. Do you have an entire semester to do the policy brief? Does your instructor expect a thorough and detailed paper (sometimes referred to by students as an issue *long* rather than an issue *brief!*) as opposed to a summary and concise analysis of the issue? What percentage of your grade depends on the project? Such questions should be put to the instructor if there is any doubt about broadening or narrowing the topic and how much work your team is expected to put into the project. Know the expectations and parameters first; decide to broaden, narrow, redefine, or switch afterwards.

We have said that changes in the topic should be communicated to the instructor. How and when should this communication take place? Will a memo be necessary, or will a quick word after class suffice? Should you set up an appointment and fully explain the problem, or is it sufficient to make a brief update report?

Normally, small revisions in the topic are expected and do not need to be reported to the instructor in great detail, provided that you document the evolution of the topic in the final report.

If you are uncertain about the direction your topic is heading, or if you experience serious frustration about the amount and quality of information you find in your preliminary review, then it's worthwhile to seek your instructor's counsel. If your team is radically revising or abandoning a topic, it's a good idea to get the instructor's permission.

You decide when and how to contact the instructor, but be *certain* that the instructor knows how you have altered the topic, since you do not want to do a great deal of work only to have the instructor say: "Why did you do *that* when I assigned *this*?"

## EXPLORING THE TOPIC THROUGH PUBLISHED LITERATURE

Preliminary literature searches are necessary to get an idea of the amount and kinds of information available on your topic. As a result of such a search, you should arrive at a fairly good conception of how much work will be needed to review, sort, analyze, and write up the information you locate. This search is not initially thorough, although it should be more or less systematic. You must start somewhere, and, presuming that you know little about the topic, you should look in some obvious places to get underway. At this initial stage, you do not want to go into any detailed analysis of information, yet you must do some tentative analysis just to assess the quantity and quality of information available.

### Taking Preliminary Notes

It makes sense to keep reference notes on information that you find in this preliminary stage. The more systematic the notes are, the better off your team will be in the long run. Ideally, a note card should be made for every source located, with notations kept for every source examined. Why look twice in the same place? Figure 4.1 shows what a well-designed note card might look like.

Notes or note cards should list the author, title, book call number, other sources (newspaper, magazine, journal, and so on) along with a capsule summary of the document. This capsule can be written by merely skimming the document for

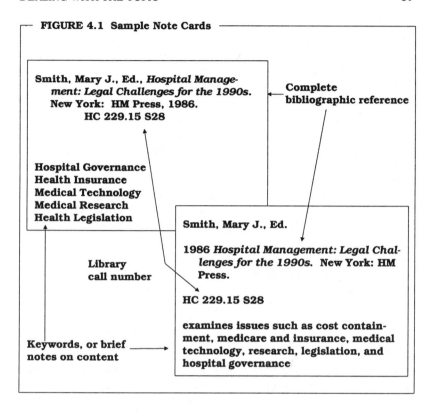

FIGURE 4.1 Sample Note Cards

the following information: (1) major themes, arguments, or questions explored; (2) evidence presented or reviewed; (3) methodology of the study (if there is one); and (4) major findings and conclusions. If you are using more than one library, or a vast library with many sections, you can also note on the card where the material was found.

## Scanning

At this stage of research, you want to be able to scan documents so that you know what they contain, without reading every word in them (you will have to go back and read many of them more thoroughly in the next phase of the project). Several methods exist for scanning documents.

If there is an *executive summary* or an *introduction*, where one can gain a good idea of the scope, questions, methods, and findings of the study, this may be all you need to read in the preliminary stage. If the document does not have a clear or thorough summary (actually, even if it does), examine the *table of contents* to see if the document covers pertinent issues. If you find something that looks relevant, turn to those chapters and read a paragraph or two from several pages to see if the treatment of the issues bears on your topic. You may also read the first chapter's introductory paragraphs and then the conclusion. If you can speed read, or scan rapidly for major ideas, this is excellent for preliminary searches as long as you are certain that you are locating the major ideas and not passing over them.

Search the *subject index*— if the document has one— and examine those pages that contain topics relevant to your project. Finally, examine the *reference or bibliography sections* and the *footnotes*. Have you never read a list of references in the back of a book or article? Do you skip the footnotes because they're so boring? Use this project as an opportunity to learn to use sources like these— as any good detective would— that will lead you to additional relevant documents and ideas.

### What to Expect in the Preliminary Search

Your aim in this preliminary stage is to map out the terrain, and to begin to get a big picture of the topic and what must be considered in analyzing it. You thus begin to get a better definition of the topic and all that it involves, particularly whether the topic needs to be narrowed or broadened. This initial research and problem refinement sets up the dynamic process between how you define the topic and what you know about it, a process that will go on far into the project and in some instances will continue all the way through to your final conclusions.

In the preliminary research stage, you are not seeking absolute certainty, clarity, and intellectual mastery on the topic. You can expect to find ambiguities, inconsistencies, puzzles, and confusions at this stage, for they are what make you think and learn as you address them. In a preliminary search, your prime task is to locate, scan, and sketch an outline of the information that is available. Secondarily, some preliminary analysis of materials automatically springs from these activities.

If the topic needs narrowing or broadening, your team should recognize this toward the end of the preliminary phase as you naturally shift from mapping out the terrain to a more detailed study of source materials. It is possible that radical topic redefinition may be needed at this time, but more likely this will occur (if at all) when you dig deeper into the evidence and begin serious analysis of the topic. If preliminary efforts are turning up little to work with, you may begin to consider switching the topic; before you come to this point, however, reread Chapter 6, where we discuss research as a detective game. You may be looking for your lost keys under the lamp-post, because that's where the light is best.

A note of caution: halfhearted efforts at preliminary literature searches produce incomplete and unsatisfying results. In most instances the statement that "there's nothing on this topic" is an indication that you have not looked deeply enough or in the right places. Remember that modern society has a great deal more information than anyone knows what to do with. There is so much information available that you need to develop skill in *learning how* to sift through it all to find what is germane to your task. Many of the brightest students tell us that knowing how and where to find information is a major time-consuming obstacle in their work.

## Use the Librarian

You already know you'll have to use the library. But you may not know that the most valuable resource (beyond your team members) that you have in locating information is a competent *librarian.* Many students are reluctant to ask a librarian for assistance; and often students will seek help from a student working at the library, mistakenly believing that a student aide knows as much as a professional librarian does, or that the librarian doesn't want to be bothered.

It has been a very long time since librarians were the people who kept the books from being damaged and shushed you if you made too much noise. Good librarians are now trained in information sciences, and they can save you a great deal of time and be a source of ideas for locating information and other related resources. Especially important is the fact that they know the intricacies and potentials of the library they work in and probably those of several other related libraries as well. Keep in mind that locating information is their profession and they are usually quite pleased to show off their skills in information retrieval. Do not be shy about making an appointment with a librarian, and be prepared to take good notes, as ideas and sources are likely to flow rapidly. Above all, remember that your team's scarcest resource is time, and a librarian can save your time. The operative ground rule is this: librarians will not do the analysis for you, but they can serve as a source of advice on how to locate information.

If there is more than one library relevant to your research (such as a public administration library, economics library, business library, government documents depository), consider dividing up the assignment among team members so that each of you interviews at least one librarian. Everyone needs the experience, and no one should be saddled with the entire library burden.

**Make Use of Experts**

An expert, someone who knows a great deal about your issue, can also save you time. Such a person can offer ideas, inside information, and advice on sources of information. It may be a member of Congress or a congressional staff person, a noted scholar in the area of your topic, a corporate strategist, a public affairs person at an organization, a journalist, or a lobbyist. Whomever it might be, do not be shy about contacting them to get started. The worst that can happen is nothing, or maybe a brushoff (which in small doses is probably good for our characters). Most experts are glad to assist eager students because they like to share what they know and they like to have people pay them the honor of considering them experts. Without doubt some experts do not want to be bothered by students, but in our experience they are uncommon. In addition to saving you time, an expert can provide insights you would have difficulty reaching on your own.

When contacting an expert at the beginning of your research, make it clear that you are getting started— do not act as if you know more than you do— and that the person's aid and suggestions would be invaluable to your team's efforts. Before going to meet with experts, ask them for homework assignments to get you familiar with the topic. If you contact experts well into the project, be prepared to tell them what you already know, *if* you are asked. The main points are to be grateful for the assistance and not to pretend you know more than you do. Experts are *supposed* to know more than you do, so let them!

### TEAM TASKS: DIVIDING THE LABOR AND UNDERSTANDING THE TOPIC

There is no ideal division of labor that will work for every team. We assume that your team will work within some model of democratic principles. Operationally, what the teams need in the preliminary research phase is an inventory of their skills and preferences for which portions of the work they want to do. Underlying this is the shared trust that no matter how the work is assigned, it will be allocated fairly.

As an example, suppose that no one wants to search government documents (affectionately known as Dox), yet this is vital to your preliminary research. If there is a member who has experience with government documents, this teammate may offer to do it and let the others know that this is a way of illustrating commitment to the team. This member may even say "you owe me one," and try to extract some favor or leniency later in the project. This is fine as long as the Dox searcher realizes that making this effort now is not an excuse from critical work (such as analysis) later in the project and does not allow a laggard approach later with the excuse that this unpleasant task was done earlier. Buy your teammate an ice cream cone, offer high praise for doing the dirty work, but do not let the member think credits have been earned toward working less later in the project. Every team member will have to participate in the preliminary research if it is to be done well, and government documents are really no harder to deal with than are the periodical indexes, the card catalog, electronic data bases, and other information sources.

Another possible response to this example is for the member experienced in searching government documents to offer to take the lead and show other team members how to access the Dox library. In this fashion, your team's expert is able to guide the work while having some help in getting it done. Another option is to have a member chime in: "I've been putting it off, but I need to learn how to use government documents." Any of these solutions is acceptable as long as all members feel that no members are taking advantage of the team.

Dividing the labor is central in dealing with the topic. Usually, the chief concerns of the team are the efficiency and effectiveness of its work. This means that you should have a good idea of the capabilities and interests of your teammates to guide your task assignments so that the project work is done quickly and well. A caveat in is order, however. Efficiency and effectiveness are undeniably good objectives, but your team must not overlook the issues of fairness and trust. It may be very efficient to "let George do it" (all the government documents searching) while the others avoid it like the plague. But is George showing signs of feeling exploited? Will George extract promises that other team members consider unfair? Will George stop working after his preliminary contribution is made?

As always, be aware of the troubles that free riders (those who are glad to do as little as possible) are likely to pose in this early stage of the project. A free rider can dampen the enthusiasm of other teammates, make promises that won't be kept, or merely bow out of doing any of the work, leaving all tasks for others. How do you know if you've got a free rider in the group? A free rider is the one who says: "Gee, I can't make that meeting, or this one, or that one," or the clever, "How 'bout if you guys do this stage and I'll type the report at the end," or the more hostile, "I don't give a ____ about this project; you can do what you want." If you have free riders, deal with them now, gently but firmly, not later when so much work has been done and bitter recriminations are the most likely result.

As for the leadership issue, your team by this point will have settled into a routine for leadership and all that it entails. If this routine works, good. If there are signs of conflict that may go on and on without resolution, showing that your team's approach to leadership may be inadequate, now is the time to settle the matter. Assuming your team has no serious problems with group dynamics, you arrive at this stage naturally, flowing into dividing the work of the entire project.

Above all, as with every aspect of the process, strive for coordination of efforts and good team-wide communication at this preliminary phase of dealing with the topic. Ask yourselves:

- ❏ Does your team feel good about itself and the topic? Is the mood of the group normally upbeat?
- ❏ Do you have a sense of direction, of how to go about producing a successful issue brief?
- ❏ Are your meetings productive and to the point?
- ❏ Are all members pulling their weight?
- ❏ Does the topic seem clearer and more manageable than it did before the preliminary research started? (If not, find out why, or see the instructor if you are lost or stumped.)
- ❏ Does the team think it needs to radically redefine or switch the topic? (Again, see the instructor if the answer is yes.)

Once you satisfy yourself on these points, you are prepared to move from dealing with the topic in a preliminary way into the more detailed work of thoroughly researching and preparing an issue brief. Although it may not necessarily be crystal clear at this time, you should have a good initial grasp of your issue. If you do not, then you are still in the preliminary stage of dealing with the topic, and what is required is one or more of the following:

- ❏ More preliminary research on the topic. Perhaps you do not have enough information on the issue to work with.
- ❏ Consideration of questions about narrowing, broadening, or re-defining the topic.
- ❏ Questions about how the group is functioning, especially: are members doing their share and really trying to explore the issue?
- ❏ A discussion with the instructor where you lay out what you have done and the difficulties you are having.

Assuming that your team has a good grasp of the topic, you can mark the transition from one stage to the next by having a meeting that pulls things together and summarizes where you stand. It is time for the team to consider what has been done, what you have learned so far, and where you need to go.

At this stage, a *work plan* is an ideal way of summarizing past efforts and gains, and pointing to the tasks that still lie ahead. A written work plan will help keep the team on target, on schedule, and continuously aware of where it has been and where it is headed. Further, it is a way of visibly setting forth the team's contractual agreement. Finally, developing a work plan indicates a professional approach to the project, and is very good experience in planning and monitoring a set of project objectives.

A work plan involves specifying which team members will do which tasks, how long it will take to do these tasks, and how the information obtained or the task accomplished flows into the next project tasks. The work plan will look something like a flow

**FIGURE 4.2 Team Work Plan (Members: Renee, Martin, Victoria, Li Jian, Hans)**

| | WEEK | | | | | |
|---|---|---|---|---|---|---|
| TASK | 1 | 2 | 3 | 4 | 5 | 6 |
| Preliminary Research | all | | | | | |
| Specific Research #1 | Renee, Martin | Renee, Martin | | | | |
| Specific Research #2 | Victoria, Li Jian | Victoria, Li Jian | | | | |
| Specific Research #3 | Hans | Hans | | | | |
| Interviewing | | Renee, Hans, Victoria | | | | |
| Analysis & Synthesis | | | Li Jian, Martin | all | | |
| Presentation Graphics | | | | Victoria Hans | | |
| Practicing the Oral Presentation | | | | | all | |
| Writing the Issue Brief | | | | all | all | |
| Producing the Issue Brief | | | | | | Martin, Renee |

chart, with checkpoints and timelines for the team as a whole and for each member. It is easy to subdivide the work plan so that it contains the chores of members and their expected contributions. Figure 4.2 presents an example of a team's work plan.

### CONCLUSION

In this chapter we have examined the main issues of dealing with the topic: redefining, narrowing, or broadening. And we have considered some of the more important group dynamics aspects that are likely to arise in this early phase of the project. If all is well— or well enough to justify going on to digging deeper into research— read on. If your team is experiencing serious difficulties with group dynamics (such as disruptive conflict over the division of labor, members not making meetings or doing assigned work) or with locating information, or with the nature of the problem, do not overlook these matters with the attitude that it will work itself out.

By this time your team has established a working style, even if it is not to work too much! The team must examine its working style to see if it will allow project objectives to be met and team members to remain on board. You also should know how much information is out there for your topic; if you have not really looked and don't know what's available, that is a problem in itself. Finally, you should have gained enough perspective on your topic to have a sense of whether it needs narrowing, broadening, or switching.

Virtually all of the teams we have worked with have problems in the preliminary stage of research. By no means should you think that any difficulty is now a disaster! Expect and value problems; they make you think and learn. Team projects are inherently problem generating, so the question is not: do you have problems? but, what are you doing to manage your problems?

# 5
## HOW TO DO A PRELIMINARY LITERATURE SEARCH

The central aim of the preliminary literature search is to allow your team to map the terrain and make the first steps in refining the topic. This means you are not going into great depth; rather you are searching for the *breadth* of the information on the topic, scanning and taking notes on documents you will return to when the research and analysis deepen.

This chapter provides you with the basic tools needed to do a preliminary literature search. You will investigate the choice to search for information manually, in printed catalogs and bibliographies, or electronically, in *computerized data bases*. You will learn how to use a card catalog and how to deal with subject headings. Journals and other printed materials are likely to be very useful, and you'll learn how to find them and access them. Finally, reference books and government documents are examined.

When you begin your search for research materials, you will face a perhaps unexpected question: whether you will use manual searching through card catalogs and bound indexes, or electronic searching via computer, or both. You may have no choice if there are no computer data bases (also known as *electronic* or *automated data bases*) available to search, or if the expense, inadequacy, or inconvenience of the electronic search is prohibitive. The advances in electronic technology are making computer searching commonplace at universities. As a general rule, computer searches are superior to manual ones, primarily because they are more systematic, more thorough, and take less time than manual searching. But be prepared to break this rule by also using manual searching, for it can serve you in ways that computer searching cannot.

Electronic searches are expensive, and they do exactly what you tell them to do, nothing more. So, if you are just beginning a search and you don't really know which subject headings to look under (that is, you're going fishing in the library), it is best to search manually first and then to move on to an electronic search once you know where you should be looking. Also, there are special conditions where manual searching is superior to computer searching (more on this later). Above all, find out *how many years* are covered by the electronic data base you are considering. As we write, many electronic indexes and catalogs at universities are incomplete, only going back a limited number of years and containing fewer of the materials by a given author or under a subject heading than are actually in the library.

Now let's go into a consideration of the various places to look, either electronically or manually. A place most students begin searching is the *card catalog*, or, as is becoming more common, *the electronic catalog* at the library. (Note that we will talk about cards as though you were going to use only a manual search. The correct term for an electronic data base is *records*.) This is as good a place as any to start, as long as you don't treat it as the only or even the primary place to look. In addition to the card catalog, there is the government documents portion of the library (a formidable source of information),[1] and indexes of journals and magazines, newspapers, statistical reports, dissertation abstracts, and much more.

## THE CARD CATALOG

What can a card catalog (manual or electronic) do for you? It is an inventory of a *significant* amount of the holdings of the library. Normally, the catalog will include listings of books, reference materials, conference reports, reports of associations and organizations, and journal titles.

The card catalog typically does not include government documents, which have their own indexes. Nor does it contain information on the contents of specific journals, dissertation abstracts, or statistical reporting services, among others. And the catalog will not mention certain holdings of the library that are too cumbersome to catalog, such as newspaper clipping files, or artworks, manuscripts, letters, and other historical documents in special collections.

When you search the card catalog you will find published books and reports on the topic *as you define it* that are in *this* library's collection. Every item is listed three times, under the headings of: (1) author's name, (2) title of the book, and (3) subject heading (as in "waste disposal" or "welfare").

Card catalogs are a primary source for locating books and reference materials on topics (by title, author, or subject heading), but the card catalog is only the first step, and an incomplete one, in preparing an issue brief. Keep in mind that you may well have a topic, either one in strategic management or public policy, where much of the information you need is found in government documents, business- and public-policy journals, corporate annual reports, congressional hearings and legislation, nonprofit institute reports, and other such materials not listed in the card catalog. It is common for students doing policy research to locate most of their information in sources other than the card catalog.

Students sometimes think that by searching one library's card catalog, they have learned all there is to know on their topic. In a policy issue brief, this is a serious misconception. So, the first caution is that in searching the card catalog, you are finding out about some books, some reports, and some reference materials. Second, and often overlooked by students, is that different libraries have different holdings, so that searching one library does not mean that you've checked on all the books that exist on your topic. For instance, if a university has a business library, its holdings will be substantially different from those of the general library or the public policy library. Search all the relevant libraries, taking advantage of the librarian's knowledge of resources available on campus and in the area. In addition, most libraries subscribe to an interlibrary loan service, so you need not feel restricted to using only the materials found in your local library.

A potential time saver is found in searching a master card (or electronic) catalog system, which catalogs the holdings of several or all libraries on campus. In this way you only have to search once to cover several or all important libraries. Most campus-based electronic catalogs include this university-wide integration (and some libraries catalog the holdings of every library in the state or region). A librarian or library assistant should be able to tell you the scope and location of the master library catalog, and many electronic catalogs offer you this information on the screen as you get started or give you the name of the library where each book is located.

## Subject Headings

If you have a book title or the name of an author, then obviously you look up the name or title as a way to get started. If, however, you do not have author names or book titles to begin with, you must rely on subject heading searches.

Your topic is likely to be cataloged under several different subject headings. For example, if you are concerned with how electronic technology (computers) in the workplace affects the nature of work, you will find little of relevance if you merely consult the catalog by looking under the headings "computers" or "computers and work." It is not that literature is not available, but that works bearing on this topic are found under various subject headings, for example, "information theory/sciences," "technology and work," "organizational behavior," "organization effectiveness," "sociology of work," and others. If you don't find references under one subject heading, try to think of how your topic fits into categories you have not explored. Once you begin to locate books, the references and bibliographies in them will lead you to other books and perhaps to other subject headings.

Many libraries have a subject headings guidebook at or near the card catalog or the terminals where you search the card catalog electronically. As an example, those libraries that use the Library of Congress's classification system have a subject heading guidebook where you look up a topic to see if it is one of the library's main subject headings (that is, a word or phrase you can use to look up books on your topic). If it is a subject heading, you then look it up in the card catalog, manually or electronically. If it is not a subject heading, the guide may refer you to the subject headings that are used to classify materials on that topic. For instance, if you are researching the American civil rights movement, the guide will inform you to "see also" such headings as "civil liberation movements," "liberation movements," "protest movements," and "social movements."

You may have to spend some time thinking about and tinkering with the various subject headings your topic comes under before you find any literature on it.  Or you may find all you need by merely looking up your topic (or authors or titles) in the card catalog.  Note, though, that it is easier to search for pertinent subject headings manually in the subject headings book than to do so on the computer, because it is simpler and faster to scan printed pages.

In addition, the card catalog is less likely to give you a dose of information overload if you don't know exactly what you're looking for yet.  If you were to ask a major electronic data base to list materials on "labor," for example, the data base would dutifully crank out the 20,000 or so references it includes under that general heading.  This would encompass perhaps 1,500 pages of printout— certainly more than you or your team want to search in the preliminary stage of your work!

The information given to you on the cards for each book you locate may look dry and boring, but it is your starting point.  Study the card or electronic record, and observe that it lists several topic headings under which the book, and others related to it, are cataloged.  This can lead you to other subject headings you might never have thought of.  For instance, one book we know of on the implications of the proliferation of personal computers and information in general is also classified under the headings of "boredom" and "information overload." Additionally, a vital step that is sometimes overlooked is the simple act of writing down the call number of the book and the library where it is located.  You can't find the book without it!

Finally, when you go to the book stacks to search for books, look at other books in the area, since call numbers are assigned according to the major subject heading under which the book is classified.  As an example, if you are interested in the policies and activities of presidents of the United States, you might start by looking up one president, say Jimmy Carter, and noting that several books on his presidency have Library of Congress call numbers beginning "E876."  When you go to this section of the library, you will find many books on the presidencies of Carter, Ronald Reagan, Richard Nixon, and so on. (The precise call numbers may vary slightly but at least you are in the ballpark and can scan the shelves fruitfully.) In this way you may track down quite an array of books on your subject.

It is so important to keep records of which libraries you have searched and the headings you have searched under! You will be amazed how quickly you forget what seems so easy to remember as you are doing the search. Why do it twice?

Furthermore, compile a collective source bibliography within the team so that you may share your information with each member. This also reduces or eliminates repetitious work. If you can keep this critical information in order on scraps of paper, use them, but a set of note cards or an indexed tablet or an electronic data base of your own are the best ways to keep this information orderly and secure. Perhaps one person in the team should be in charge of keeping a master reference list and the others should actively update this list as they report to the team on their individual research efforts.

To guide your search through card catalogs (either manual or electronic), ask yourself these questions on behalf of the team:

- ❑ Have we searched under all possible subject headings?
- ❑ Have we used the sources we've already located to point to more sources?
- ❑ Think about the library itself: what kind of library is it— the main one at a major university? a specialized one (for example, economics or law) at a university? a local city library? Should we search other libraries or more comprehensive catalogs for books on our topic?
- ❑ Is the electronic catalog we used a complete listing of the library's holdings? If not, what's missing?
- ❑ Where do we go from here? (for you're not finished— you have just begun).

It is possible that when you finish your preliminary catalog search, you may be very disappointed that you have found little or nothing; you should know, however, that in policy research, this is quite common. If this happens to you, you are not yet ready to switch topics or to conclude that no information exists on your topic; you are only ready to look in other places, to which we turn now.

## JOURNALS, REPORTS, AND ABSTRACTS

Staple sources for published information include academic and scholarly journals, newspapers, popular and trade periodicals,

and a host of regular or occasional publications from foundations, institutes, businesses, trade associations, statistical abstracting services, dissertation abstract services, and the
government.  Most of these materials are cataloged in one or
more indexes available in libraries and, as is becoming common,
many libraries are developing or adopting these indexes in
electronic formats.   Not all of these materials are available
electronically at present, so bear in mind that you may have to
search both manually and electronically to thoroughly explore
the indexes relevant to your topic.  The variations in library
capabilities are too great to do more than alert you to this state
of affairs.

**Electronic Searching**

For now, let's assume that you are considering electronic searching.  There are a multitude of electronic indexes on the market,
far too many to list here, so what should you do?  Here is a
checklist of considerations to apply as you search electronic data
bases.  Some data bases are more powerful than others and you
should know the basic differences lest you search with a weak
one and miss finding information on your topic.  (A powerful
data base is one that is designed to provide sophisticated
information retrieval to unsophisticated users. That is, it's easy
to use and does a lot for you.)  A librarian can guide you on this
matter. If a librarian is not available, keep in mind these factors
about electronic searching of data bases:

1.  *Access*: is it open or restricted (that is, do you need an appoint-
    ment and is your time limited?)
2.  *Cost*: must you pay for searching the electronic data base?
3.  *Conducting the search*: can you do it yourself, or must a profes-
    sional operator do it for you with subject headings (topical key
    words) you provide?
4.  *Turnaround time*: can you get the search information on the spot
    or must you wait for it? Do you have to pick up the results (output
    or printout), or will the library mail or deliver them to you?
5.  *Search protocols or routines*:  Do you know how to search the data
    base?  If not, is it easy to learn?  Does the data base give you
    simple instructions as you use it?  If not, plan to be versed in how
    to search before you begin, unless you know you can learn as you

go without penalty (that is, in terms of money, time for others to use the system, and so on).

6.  *Power of the search:* some electronic data bases only search by a single key word (title, name, or subject), while others are quite sophisticated and can search by topic areas and by subtopics (delimited or narrowed searches, such as "business and political action"). It's a good idea to know the capabilities of the system on which you are searching.

7.  Which *sources* are indexed in the data base? Not all data bases index identical holdings. There are any number of specialized data bases (such as in management documents, book reviews, statistical reports, environmental affairs, newspapers, and so on), and it is up to you to know what each data base indexes (the names of journals, magazines, newspapers, and so forth). Most fields of study have their own data bases and manual abstracting indexes, such as *Psychological Abstracts, Business Periodicals Index,* and *Public Affairs Information Services.*

There are any number of data bases available to you either electronically or manually with vastly differing search capabilities, indexes of holdings, and demands on the user. It is virtually a requirement— especially if you are having difficulty finding information— for your team to find out about how electronic search systems work and what they contain so that you may use them to your advantage. It is of no matter if your teammates have reservations about electronic searches or preferences for searching manually (through bound indexes). Once learned and understood, computer searching is usually superior to manual searching. It is not difficult to learn once the psychological barriers are hurdled, and it is a skill that will serve you well throughout your professional life.

## Manual Searching

You may not have access to computer data bases, and you probably won't find everything you need on an electronic data base anyway. Therefore, you should be aware that manual searching isn't necessarily something you do instead of electronic searching. Manual searching has special advantages over, or is a complement to, computer searching.

The sheer number of indexing services (of materials not included in the card catalog) is impressive and too large to give separate mention to each index here. Therefore, we will offer some general comments designed to get readers past any psychologically intimidating fears they may have, which are common when faced with row upon row of indexes.

## Indexes

If you walk into any well-stocked university library, on its first floor you typically will see many rows of indexes on a truly wide range of areas. To name but a few, these will probably include: *Dissertation Abstracts*, the *Reader's Guide to Periodical Literature*; the *Biography Index*, the *Statistical Reference Index*, the *Public Affairs Information Services Index*, the *Social Science Citation Index*, *Sociological Abstracts*, *Psychological Abstracts*, *Business Periodicals Index*, the *Book Review Digest*, the *Environmental Index*, and the list could go on and on.

The first thing to know is that once you get the hang of them, indexes become handy and efficient ways of searching, although there is no doubt that some are easy to use while others are more demanding if you wish to use them to full benefit. Let's spend a moment going over how to use them. Some, like the *Reader's Guide to Periodical Literature*, are very easy to use: you merely look up a word topic (subject or name) and, if it has appeared in a title or as a main subject in an article in any of the periodicals indexed by the *Reader's Guide*, there will be a reference directing you to the magazine or journal. The *Reader's Guide* does not provide an abstract (that is, a short summary) of articles, it merely tells you where to look for articles containing the word or name you searched under. A cumbersome feature of this index is that you must search it on a year-by-year basis, that is, each year is contained in a separate volume. In the front of this index you will find a list of all the periodicals indexed in the *Reader's Guide*, which are almost exclusively popular and other nontechnical periodicals.

There are other indexes that do provide abstracts of articles. They are beneficial because you can read the abstracts and then decide whether you want to go to the trouble of looking up the entire article. *Sociological Abstracts*, for example, can be searched by word topic, author's name, or subject area. Because it includes abstracts, it has two parts. The first part is a book of word topics and author names (which provides abstract numbers to direct you to the abstracts), and the second part is a book with the abstracts. You may search by word topic (subject) or by name or you may go directly to the abstracts, where they are divided into main topical areas such as "sociology of work and occupations," "social problems," and so on. You can browse the sociology abstracts by scanning all the article abstracts in a given subject area. As an example, if you are looking for articles on computers and work, the "sociology of work and occupations" topical area of the *Sociological Abstracts* is worth examining since it will contain an abstract of all articles written on the subject, that is, all the articles in journals that are indexed in *Sociological Abstracts*.

As a primary source of tracking how policy issues develop, and for the amount of depth given to many issues, especially those involving governmental activities, *The New York Times* is a very useful resource. This newspaper publishes its own index which lists every story it prints, no matter how small. As an example of its usefulness to you, The *New York Times* regularly prints excerpts or occasionally the entire text of presidential speeches, testimony before congressional hearings, and similar matters deemed of significant public importance. This index is an excellent tool for developing a quick scan of the chronology of events and actions surrounding an issue as well as an occasional source for a detailed analysis of stakeholders and their positions.

Every index has a *user's guide* in its front section where instructions are provided on how to use the index; some are very easy to use and others will take some time to master. As noted above, the *Reader's Guide to Periodical Literature* is easy to use. In contrast, the *Social Science Citation Index* is rather difficult to use, but this citation index can be well worth the time it requires to learn how to use it. We will return to using this index later, since it probably will not come into play frequently in a preliminary literature search.

A thirty-minute glance through several of these indexes will give you an appreciation of what they can do for you. Since they cover such an array of topics, just by glancing over them you should see some indexes that will provide further sources for your preliminary search. Each index addresses a special body of information sources (periodicals, journals, foundation reports, and various other published materials), which means that you will have to look for the right indexes for your needs. In most instances, however, preliminary searches on public policy will attain best results from the *Public Affairs Information Services Index*, and in strategic management from the *Business Periodicals Index*. There is some overlap in these indexes, but for the most part, each is a specialized set of sources.

Take your time to be certain that you have the correct indexes to work with. Do not be inhibited from using ones that seem too hard to deal with, for the ultimate aim is to find pertinent information, and not to be surprised by learning later in the project that you have overlooked an arena of vital information.

## REFERENCE BOOKS

Another valuable source of materials is found in the reference section of the library. Reference books are listed in the card catalog, but it is difficult to find them by looking them up in the card catalog if you do not know their specific names. Given this problem, we provide a few reference source names, descriptions, and call numbers here to familiarize you with the reference section of the library. (Most larger libraries have a reference librarian who specializes in retrieving information from these sources; if your library does not, ask the head librarian for help.)

What makes a book a reference book? In a broad sense, a *reference book* is a book that the library considers so important to all users that the book is not allowed to circulate (to be checked out); it must remain in the library, where users have access to it at all times. Several kinds of books can be classified as reference books, such as who's-who books of famous people in a profession, books with statistical information, books that describe or catalog types of organizations (as in the *Foundations Directory*), or books that contain encyclopedic knowledge (as in the various *Encyclopedias of...*).

Reference books do have call numbers, and this is of special interest to you. By looking in the area of a given call number, which you have already identified through your preliminary card catalog search, useful reference books on the topic may be found. For instance, if your library uses the Library of Congress call numbering system, the letter *H* is a general heading for books in the social sciences (including much of the work done in business and public policy). Without knowing the titles or authors of any reference books, you may go to the reference section of the library and begin to look through the *H* section of reference books to see what you can find related to your topic.

Here are some (by no means all) of the handy reference books you would find. Under the call number "R HA 202 S84" (the *R* designates this as a reference book) you would find the U.S. Department of Commerce's publication, *State and Metropolitan Area Data Book*, and in this book you will find a variety of useful statistical information divided by the 50 states and metropolitan areas of the United States.[2] These data include crime, health care, vital statistics, housing, and manufacturing among 36 categories included therein. Under the number "R HF5353 B717" you would find Brownstone and Carruth's *Where to Find Business Information*, a very useful guide to subjects and publishers in business, finance and related matters;[3] another such reference book there is Lorna M. Daniels, *Business Information Sources*.[4] Three more handy sources which cover business, scientific, professional, and trade societies are, Gale Research of Detroit's *Directory of Directories*, the *Encyclopedia of Associations*, and the *Encyclopedia of Business Information Sources*.[5] As you scan the *H* section, you would come also across Chase and Tuttle's *Information Sources*, under the number "R HC102 I53".[6] These reference books include sources (topical areas) and publishers of business information. Brownstone and Carruth's book also tells the reader how much the information costs, if anything, to obtain.

Rather than capsulize the many guidebooks available, we will list a few of the most significant ones before moving on. These include: the *Guide to American Directories*, B. Klein Publications; *How to Find Information About Companies*, Donna M. Jablonski, ed.; *How to Win with Information or Lose Without It*, by A. P. Garvin and H. Bermont; the *Organizations, Agencies, and Publishers Directory*, A.T. Kruzas and L. Varekamp Sullivan, eds.[7] Two more how-to books bear mentioning because they provide detail about finding sources and data. They are *How to Use the Business Library: With Sources of Business Information*, by H.W. Johnson, A.J. Faria and E.L. Maier, and *Secondary Research: Information Sources and Methods* by D.W. Stewart.[8]

## GOVERNMENT DOCUMENTS

Some students dread the prospect of going through government documents. We recognize that a sense of resolve is needed to take on this chore, for the Dox section (as government documents are unaffectionately known) in some ways reflects the complexity of our society. Approaching government documents can be like getting psyched up to dive into the swimming pool when you know the water is chilly. Yet once you dive in and get used to it, you find satisfaction in mastering, or at least coping with, the intricate world of government documents.

For some policy briefs, the use of government documents may be minimal or unnecessary. For most public policy issues, however, some or extensive use of them is required. The effort is worth it, and for many topics it is indispensable, since it is here that most of your information will be found.

This discussion is based on our experiences working with government documents and on the thorough book by Edward Herman, entitled *Locating United States Government Information: A Guide to Sources*.[9] A primary misunderstanding of government documents concerns what exactly they are. As Herman notes, many people:

> . . . have an incorrect conception of the kinds of materials published by the United States government. They believe documents are limited to laws, regulations, court decisions, and loads of statistics. In reality, federal publications cover all subjects from A through Z. The National Aeronautic and Space Administration's volumes incorporate beautifully illustrated color plates of photographs taken from spacecrafts . . . the Department of Justice publishes public opinion surveys about crime, and the House Government Operations Committee publishes hearings on the safety of intrauterine contraceptive devices. . . . [There are] thousands more just as diverse, interesting, and informative . . . government documents.

Once you begin to search in the several indexes and catalogs of government documents, you will see this diversity for yourself. A second useful book on using government documents developed for those examining issues in a business context is, *A Handbook for Business on the Use of Federal and State Statistical Data*, by E. G. May.[10]

Some basic information on government documents is needed for those new to them. All libraries do not collect them, and not all government documents are available at the libraries that do collect them. It works like this. The U. S. government designates various libraries throughout the country as depository libraries and gives free copies of selected documents to them regularly, with the understanding that these documents are freely available to all patrons. Herman informs us that as of 1980, there were more than 1,300 depository libraries in the United States, mostly found at major universities and in mid-size and large cities.

Many libraries will have some government documents, but only a depository library will have an adequate range of documents for policy research. So, if your issue brief requires extensive use of government materials, you will need to locate the depository library nearest you, and make use of it and its documents librarian.

A central source of problems with government documents is their sheer volume. There are just too many documents, with more arriving continuously, to include in the main card catalog of a library. As Herman tells us, the Government Printing Office in Washington, D.C. is the largest publisher in the world. Because of this, only a few major government documents (often standard reference volumes like the annual *Statistical Abstracts of the United States*) are included in most main library card catalogs. The vast majority of documents must be located by searching one of several government document indexes. Usually, but not exclusively, you will find yourself consulting the *Monthly Catalog* of *United States Government Publications* index as the most reliable and handy index of government documents.

A difficulty, although usually an insignificant one, with the *Monthly Catalog* is that it too is not a *complete* bibliographic source of all government sponsored documents, although it is inclusive enough for most research needs. Many agencies often fail to submit complete monthly lists of their publications to the Government Printing Office; hence some documents go unrecorded in the *Monthly Catalog* or are cataloged at later dates. Further, many documents are classified, that is, not available to the public. For most student researchers, these qualifications are of little importance. For some, however, they may be of special interest (see Herman's book for more on finding out about and locating such hard-to-find documents, including those that must be obtained using the procedures of the Freedom of Information Act).

## The Monthly Catalog

As noted, the *Monthly Catalog of United States Government Publications* is the primary reference source used by most researchers. It is available at all libraries that deposit government documents. It has two parts: (1) a comprehensive index referring you to entry (or document) numbers, and (2) a bibliographic section showing full reference citations by document number.

The comprehensive portion of the *Monthly Catalog* indexes documents in six different ways: by title, author, subject, series report number, stock number, and title key words. This is especially helpful for those who are beginning research and only have a subject or key word to guide them. You will find an *entry number* (for example, "78–18847") for each document. The first two digits refer to the year, in this case 1978, and the last five to the document number in the 1978 *Monthly Catalog* bibliography section.

When you look up document 18847 in the 1978 *Monthly Catalog* bibliography section, you get a document citation with all six of the indexing dimensions listed in the main index, for example, the full title, author, issuing agency, and so on. This information can allow you to branch out in your search if you start with a key word and then discover that a certain government agency or author has published additional materials on your topic.

The bibliography also gives you the information needed to tell if the document is one that is on deposit in libraries. (Do not be put off by the maze of numbers in the bibliography. An explanatory guide at the front of the *Monthly Catalog* details what each number means.) Determining if a document is on deposit in the library is done by simply looking down the left hand column of the bibliographic citation for a black dot (•) with the word *Item* after it. If the black dot and the word *Item* appear, it is a library depository document. If it is a depository document, then look up near the top of the citation (typically right below the entry number that led you to this citation) for the Superintendent of Documents Number (sometimes called the SuDox Number), which tells you where to look for the document in the government documents section of the library, not in the general stacks where books are kept. The SuDox numbers are actually a combination of letters and numbers, as in "HH 1.6/3:R 31/2/part." All these letters and numbers have a meaning, which is explained in the *Monthly Catalog* and in Herman's reference book (1983), but all you need to know to find the document now is where the stacks of government publications are located. (Some libraries restrict access to the documents section, so you may have to fill out a request form and have a library staff person bring the document to you.)

If there is no black dot by the word *Item*, it is probably not at the library. If you need it, you will have to order the document from the Government Printing Office or the issuing government agency, or search for it in another depository library, or ask to borrow it on interlibrary loan. The *Monthly Catalog* itself and Herman's book tell you how to order from the GPO. A final point is that some libraries have electronic (computerized) access to the *Monthly Catalog* and, of course, this option can be a real time saver if it is available to you.

## Other Government Documents Indexes

The *Government Printing Office Sales Publication Reference File* (short name— PRF) is precisely what its name suggests— as are the titles of most government documents— an index of government documents available for sale to the public. Herman tells us that this index, and its monthly supplement, frequently supplies information on new publications before the *Monthly Catalog* does. If you can master the use of the *Monthly Catalog*, you will be able to use the *PRF* as well.

Another helpful index is the *Cumulative Title Index To United States Documents*, which in its various volumes, indexes virtually all government publications since 1789.

The *Index To United States Government Periodicals* can be of great value, because many government periodicals (that is, publications that appear regularly, like magazines or newsletters) are not included in most periodical indexes. That is to say, you may learn of a given government periodical only by looking here. You might be surprised to learn that approximately 170 United States government periodicals are indexed here, addressing highly specialized issues in great detail. Herman informs us that the only other index that covers a large number of government documents is the *American Statistics Index*, which is not found in the government documents section of the library (it is published as a commercial venture by a company), but with the other indexes discussed earlier in this chapter.

Two other sources to cover, even though many of the periodicals they index are included in the *Index To United States*

*Government Periodicals* and the *American Statistics Index* , are the *Monthly Catalog Serial Supplement* and the *Government Periodicals and Subscription Services (GPSS)*. If you want to do a thorough job, you will need to consult all of these periodical indexes, or as many of them as you can find, especially if you are having difficulty locating enough information on your topic. Your library may not have all of these indexes, but it should have most of them.

**Bureau of the Census Publications**

The U.S. Bureau of the Census publishes a variety of documents with titles that are accurate (if boring) descriptions of what they contain. Here are several publications that may be of special value: the *Census of Populations*; the *Census of Housing;* the *Census of Retail Trade*; the *Census of Service Industries*; the *Census of Wholesale Trade*; the *Census of Manufacturers*; the *Census of Mineral Industries*; the *Census of Transportation*; the *Census of Agriculture*; *County and City Data Book*; and the *Census of Government*, which presents information on state and local governments throughout the nation.

Published annually, the invaluable *Statistical Abstract of the United States* contains summary data on demographic, economic, educational, and other significant aspects of U.S. society. When you are starting your research, this abstract may be especially useful in helping you identify the kinds of statistical information available from the government.

**Other Statistical Reports**

There are several statistical documents the government regularly releases. These include, from the Commerce Department: *Business Statistics, County Business Patterns, Survey of Current Business, Handbook of Cyclical Indicators*, the *Federal Statistical Directory*, the *State and Metropolitan Area Data Book*, the *Survey of Current Business*, and the *U.S. Industrial Outlook*. The Council of Economic Advisors has a monthly publication entitled *Economic Indicators*; the *Economic Report of the President* is an annual publication; the *Federal Reserve Bulletin* is issued monthly; the Bureau of Labor Statistics issues the *Monthly*

*Labor Review* (containing statistics of unemployment and employment, changes in the labor market, earnings, wholesale and retail prices, and work stoppages); and the Internal Revenue Service annually issues *Statistics of Income*, which covers individuals, corporations, partnerships, and sole proprietorships. Several of these publications may be found in more than one place in a library; some are listed in the main card catalog (because they are commonly sought-after references) and are classified as reference materials. The rest are indexed in the *Monthly Catalog* and perhaps other government indexes cited above. You should have no difficulty in locating any of them.

### Congressional Publications

The U.S. Congress publishes a huge volume of materials that may be relevant to your issue research. A convenient source for locating congressional publications is the *CIS Index to Publications of the United States Congress* (known simply as the *CIS*). It provides information on all major matters the Congress has covered, such as legislative and special hearings and the history of bills and legislation. The *CIS* appears in the two familiar parts, index and abstracts, titled respectively, the *Index To Congressional Publications and Public Laws*, and the *Abstracts of Congressional Publications and Legislative Histories*.

Similar to the *Monthly Catalog*, the *CIS* has six indexed sections: by subjects and names, titles, bill number, report number, document number, and committee and subcommittee chairperson's name. Each of these may prove important in your search. You should know that the *Monthly Catalog* and the *CIS* are two very commonly used indexes, and by consulting them in the preliminary research phase, you should be able to judge whether there is any readily available government information on your topic.

### PUBLICATIONS AND THE CONGRESSIONAL PROCESS

For the sake of thoroughness, there are a few more things you need to know about congressional documents. A bill introduced in Congress follows certain paths before it becomes a law (if it ever does). At each phase, Congress issues various types of

publications. Figure 5.1 shows the legislative process as de-
scribed by Herman.[11]

At this point we would like to be able to tell you that the
publications listed above are the only ones issued by the Congress, but in the complicated world of government documents,
this is not the case. They are, nonetheless, frequently used and
are an adequate guide to congressional activities.

Here is a short set of definitions of these and other congressional documents based on Herman's description of them.[12]
Bills are published according to which body of Congress, the
House or the Senate, issues them; Senate bills begin with an *S*
and House of Representatives bills begin with an *H* or, occasion-

**FIGURE 5.1 How a Bill Becomes a Law**

| THE LEGISLATIVE PROCESS | PUBLICATIONS |
| --- | --- |
| 1. Bills and resolutions are introduced in the Senate or the House of Representatives. | Bills and Resolutions |
| 2. Bills referred to committees. | Hearings |
| 3. Committees report on bills. | Reports (of the House or Senate) |
| 4. Bills are debated (in the House or Senate), and if passed, are sent to the other body (Senate or House) for consideration. | *Congressional Record* |
| 5. If bill passes both bodies, a conference committe settles differences in the two versions of the bill. | Conference report |
| 6. A compromise bill is sent back to each body for debate. | *Congressional Record* |
| 7. If passed, bill is sent to the president for approval. | |
| a. If the president signs the bill into law. | Slip law (Note: Slip laws are published by the General Services Administration, not Congress.) |
| b. If the president vetoes bill. | Veto message is published. |
| 8. Veto override: two-thirds of each body votes against the president in support of the bill. | Bill becomes law, is published as a Slip law. |

ally, *H.B.* Next, consecutive numbers indicate the order in which the bill was introduced in the Congress, along with the Congress's session number, say the one-hundreth, or the eighty-eighth. (Every two years there are elections in which the entire House and one-third of the Senate is elected. Each time these elections take place and the new members are sworn into office, the number of the Congress changes.) In the ninety-eighth Congress, the first Senate bill is S.1, and in the House it is H.1. So if you are looking for a particular bill, you must know if it is a House or Senate bill and during which session of Congress it was considered. Finally, there are joint resolutions (H.J. Res. or S.J. Res.), concurrent resolutions (H. Con. Res. or S. Con. Res.), and simple resolutions (H. Res. or S. Res.), which are also concurrently numbered by the congressional session in which they occur.

*Committee Prints* are analytic works on issues before the Congress. Herman explains that until recently these were primarily internal documents and were difficult for the public to obtain. Currently, new and recent *Committee Prints* are indexed in the *Monthly Catalog*, *PRF*, and *CIS*.

Congressional committee hearings and reports are a useful source of information as they include a verbatim transcript of discussions regarding proposed legislation and matters the committee is empowered to oversee or investigate. These hearings and reports are indexed in the three main indexing sources listed in the previous paragraph. One of the interesting features about committee hearings is that you can get a clear sense of the committee chairperson's priorities because of the order assigned to various speakers. Normally, the chairperson's favored position is presented during the first day or two of a hearing, which are often covered by the media. Opposing speakers are likely to appear on the last day of the hearing, when the press has moved on to something else and even the members of Congress send staff representatives instead of going themselves.

The *Congressional Record* is published daily while Congress is in session. It includes debates, speeches, statements, and votes, as well as documents and commentary related to matters that members of Congress ask to be included in the *Record*. This is like Congress's daily diary. A helpful section of the *Record* is the Daily Digest section, which summarizes legislative actions and hearings, and provides a schedule of hearings for the following days. This digest is a quick way to locate or get a capsule summary on an issue you are following through Congress.

At the end of each two-year session of Congress, the congressional *Journals* are issued. The *Journals* offer another quick method for tracing voting records, legislative history, presidential messages, and sundry materials.

*Congressional Documents* are not the same as government documents, discussed earlier, even though they are indexed in the *Monthly Catalog*, the *PRF* and the *CIS*. These are documents the Congress believes will be of interest to the public; as you can imagine, they cover a very wide area. *Congressional Documents* includes messages sent to Congress by the president or other government agencies, and reports by private agencies sent to Congress in the public interest.

There are some government publications— primarily materials concerning treaties— that involve only the Senate and the president and not the House of Representatives. These materials are published in either *Senate Executive Documents* or *Senate Executive Reports*. Both are indexed in the *Monthly Catalog*, the *PRF*, the *CIS*, and the *Congressional Index*.

The *Congressional Quarterly Almanac*, the *Congressional Quarterly Weekly Report*, and *Congress and The Nation* are all good sources for easily tracing an area of public policy (such as pharmaceutical regulation or white-collar crime), or the legislative history of a specific bill relating to a broad policy area (such as a proposed amendment to ban certain additives in prescription medicines or a bill requiring mandatory jail sentences for persons convicted of computer crimes). These indexes overlap in their coverage, but that is an advantage because you get to look them over and work with the ones that are easiest for you to use. Further, if you are bent on a thorough search, the indexes are not identical, so searching each one is a good idea.


## CONCLUSION

Libraries, need it be said, are there to be used, and you now have a very good idea about how to use them to conduct a preliminary search of the literature on your topic. Using the library, with its card catalogs, indexes, reference books, and government documents, seems cumbersome, arcane, and sometimes downright unfriendly to many new users. Yet once you get into the swing of it, you will find a wealth of experience and information that will deepen your knowledge, enliven your report, and give you life-long search skills.

## ENDNOTES

1. See Edward Herman, *Locating United States Government Information: A Workbook Guide* (Buffalo, NY: W.S. Hein Books), 1983.

2. U.S. Department of Commerce, *State and Metropolitan Area Data Book* (Washington, DC: U.S. Government Printing Office), annual.

3. David Brownstone and Gorton Caruthers, *Where to Find Business Information: A World-Wide Guide for Everyone Who Needs the Answers to Business Questions* (New York: Wiley and Sons), 1982.

4. Lorna Daniels, *Business Information Sources* (Berkeley, CA: University of California Press), 1985.

5. Gale Research Inc., *The Directory of Directories* (Detroit, MI: Gale Research Inc.), 1988.

6. Leslie Chase and P. Tuttle, Eds., *Information Sources* (Washington, DC: Information Industries), 1986.

7. Bernard Klein, *The Guide to American Directories* (Coral Gables, FL: Klein Publishing), annual; Donna M. Jablonski, *How to Find Information About Companies* (Coral Gables, FL: Klein Publishing), 1983; Andrew P. Garvin and Hubert Bermont, *How to Win with Information or Lose Without It* (Glenelg, MD: Bermont Books), 1985; Anthony T. Kruzas and L. Varekamp Sullivan, *Organizations, Agencies, and Publishers Directory* (Detroit, MI: Gale Research Inc.), 1984.

8. H. Webster Johnson, Anthony J. Faria, and E.L. Maier, *How to Use the Business Library: With Sources of Business Information* (San Antonio, TX: South-West Publishers), 1984; David W. Stewart, *Secondary Research: Information Sources and Methods* (Beverly Hills, CA: Sage Publications), 1985.

9. Herman, *Locating*, quotation from p. vii.

10. Elanor G. May, *A Handbook for Business on the Use of Federal and State Statistical Data* (Charlottesville, VA: Tayole Murphy Institute), 1984.

11. Herman, *Locating*, pp. 43–44.

12. Herman, *Locating*, pp. 44–48.

# 6

## GETTING SERIOUS: RESEARCH WITH PUBLISHED SOURCES

In this chapter we get more specific about how to research published sources, including a discussion of the two critical tasks at this phase, note taking and team-wide organization. Then we explore the idea of research as detective work by having you ask: have we looked everywhere? and, have we looked logically? This stage of research will take you farther into the actual analysis, so that when you come to the formal stage of putting things together in an issue brief, some of your basic headwork will have been done. Finally, we note the particular importance of group dynamics in this phase, centering on your ability to do the research thoroughly with sound coordination and logistics, which automatically leads you to begin a spirited analysis (that is, a productive conflict and debate) of the issue.

If you have employed the search activities outlined in the previous chapter, your team has a substantial or at least an adequate list or set of reference note cards on materials to begin examining in depth. It is likely you will discover more sources as you go along. Taking notes and keeping the team organized so that work is done well, and without duplication, are obviously important. Yet teams often do these jobs poorly and pay the price later, in lost effort and confusion, when the time comes to pull it all together and analyze the findings. As a logical place to begin, then, we turn to the matter of note taking, a disarmingly simple yet powerfully misunderstood activity.

### A NOTE IN THE HAND IS WORTH TWO IN THE HEAD

Note taking, as the sociologist C. Wright Mills observed, is not a thought-free activity.[1] Instead it is an active intellectual production, an activity that engages the mind.  As you take notes you are not merely acting as a transcribing machine; you are sorting, weighing, and classifying information, deciding what to write and in what order and depth to write it.  Equally important, of course, are the blanks, the things you choose not to include in your notes.

There are several ways to take good notes, and none is inherently better than the others. The broad aim of note taking is to simplify and organize information with a minimum of distortion and loss.  Difficulties for the team occur when various methods and intentions for taking notes are present among team members.  What is a good set of notes to Joe, who details every point in the document in thorough outline format, may be a ponderous and unnecessary set of notes to Tom, who just hits the high points, looks for main ideas, and assumes he will recall the rest from memory if it's really important.

The routinely asked question about note taking is: how do you do it?  But the prior question is: *why* are you taking notes? what purpose are they supposed to serve? (Your team may need to discuss this question, so don't think that it is too obvious to consider.)  When the purpose of note taking is to serve an individual's information needs, that is, when others do not have to read your writing or follow your "strange" notations or thought patterns, then all that matters is that the notes are comprehensible to you, the note taker, and that they are comprehensive in abstracting from the document what is relevant to your topic. (Incomplete notes are often disastrous, especially where each member is solely responsible for a document.)  This means that at the minimum you can read your notes and explain them to your teammates without trouble.

In a project such as this, the nature and relevance of the document to your project should direct you as to how to take notes.  Is the document very technical, with much detailed information, analysis, and qualifications of the argument and the evidence? At first, it seems that very detailed notes, or even copying of the entire document is in order. But extensive note taking or copying costs time and money and if done to excess leads to a wasteful pile of unexamined documents and notes. So, first decide how much or which portions of the document are pertinent to your topic. In other words, look the document over and ask yourself how it fits into the issue, what role it plays, before commencing note taking. This makes you think (good for analytic reasons), and it will save you time. For example, if you are studying environmental regulations governing the release of pollutants into the atmosphere, you will find many highly detailed, technically complex, and lengthy documents from government, nonprofit, and corporate organizations. Fully out-lining the contents of each document may not be required by the specific framing of your topic. On the other hand, complete notes on some of these documents may be essential to your team's research. Therefore, whatever your situation, think first, and then outline all of those sections that bear on your topic and merely (but importantly) note the other subjects covered so that you know where to return in case your analysis later requires it. In some instances, you may want to discuss docu-ments as a team before outlining them.

Try to maintain the balance between your major resource constraints, usually time and money, and your commitment to a quality product. If you had unlimited time and other needed resources, each member could follow a detailed note-taking format and then write up all of the notes and give them to the rest of the team. Most teams cannot and do not work this way, if only because time is scarce and styles of note taking are closely connected to one's personal preferences. Given this, the best approach is to come up with a team-wide set of guidelines for note taking and the organization of all the information you are covering. You should also make a discussion of each member's research activities a regular part of team meetings.

Since note-taking is an individual activity that must be transformed into a team-serving output, you have some deci-sions to reach so that the guidelines do not seem silly or burdensome to the members. You might agree that each of you has a different style— some take notes with great precision, for example, while others do not. In most cases these differences in style cannot be altered in the limited amount of time you have to work on the topic. Therefore, why not agree— and this is just a suggestion— that however each member chooses to do it, they must follow certain format rules and incorporate certain information for each document. For example:

1. *Use a standardized medium for note taking.* Do you want to do it on loose-leaf paper? Fine, do all note taking on the same type of loose-leaf paper. Better still, to avoid losing notes, how about a bound notebook? Or will you use note cards of one size? Do you want to color key types of notes? Above all, try to avoid the thousand-scraps-of-paper fiasco where notes are misplaced easily, or are difficult to keep in order.

2. *Always reference the document so it can be retraced at any time.* Write down the author or source, title, call number, and page number when taking notes. Why spend two hours trying to find a source for the second time because you didn't write the reference down the first time? Remember, your issue brief requires full referencing of sources.

3. *Summarize the entire contents.* When not taking notes on the entire document, which is common, briefly indicate what else is in the document on other subjects, or copy the table of contents (by hand or on a photocopy machine). This will save you time when, especially during the analysis phase, a new twist to the project comes up and you say: "Hey, I was looking at something that bears on that last week. Now, what was it?" Rarely do you recall just where you read it, but you have the reference in your notes, easily retrievable.

4. *Sort and file notes.* At the least, sort individual notes into categories that make sense to you and to the topic you are working on. If someone on the team is energetic and coordinated enough, this teammate can sort each member's notes into a master file. Force yourself to sort and file if it doesn't come naturally to you. Sorting is not only a good technique for organizing, keeping track of notes, and saving time, it is also an excellent and underused way to actually analyze what you have read. By sorting, you are thinking about how various pieces of information fit together. Do not worry if the categories aren't precise or if they overlap. Precision is not critical at this stage as long as you are trying to make sense of what you have read.

5. *Make sure that you can read your own writing and your shorthand symbols.* It is very common that hastily taken notes are illegible even to their author, much less to anyone else trying to use them.

**6.** *Decide what you are seeking before taking the notes.* The answer
   will guide how much and which type of detail you choose:
   (a) Sometimes you take notes to record the structure and infor-
       mation in the document; these notes reflect an attempt to
       accurately summarize. This is the familiar who? what?
       when? where? and how? approach to note taking.
   (b) Sometimes you take notes on only a portion of the document
       that bears on your topic, a short form of (a), above.
   (c) Sometimes you take notes to get ideas or to make a critical
       appraisal of the document. Thus your notes may skip around
       and not follow the organization of the document.
   (d) Note taking, of course, can include any combination of these
       three.

Those who categorize their notes are not being fastidious
or wasting precious time. Sorting and filing notes in a preliminary analysis will make the final analysis and preparation of the
issue brief easier, deeper, more coherent, and better reasoned.

The team, of course, must devise a method of sharing what
each member is learning from note taking on published sources.
A good technique is for each member to summarize researched
materials orally at group meetings and to have written notes
available for the rest of the team to read when the time comes
for them to have the more detailed information.

Occasionally, we find students who are dissatisfied with
the way they take notes. Such an elemental problem should not
go unaddressed, since the ability to take good notes is vital to
professional and intellectual performance in general. A.J.
Roth's book, *The Research Paper* (1982), has a useful chapter
entitled "Recording Information."[2] You might also take a look at
Miles and Huberman's (1984) book, *Qualitative Data Analysis*,
for ideas on systematic recording of notes, observations, and
interview data.[3]


## RESEARCH AS SLEUTHING

Let's set the stage for a research drama: as note taking progresses
and members share their findings, a consensus emerges that the
research is not turning up enough material, both in terms of
quantity and quality, on the topic. Gaping holes remain where
information is absent on central questions. The team is getting
discouraged because the research is going poorly or slowly.

Members can often be heard to lament: "There's so little on this topic! How are you ever going to get a major research project done if there's nothing to research?"

Another scenario: the team has discovered a lot of material to work with, but there are lingering doubts about the thoroughness of the search. Team members might comment: "We've found a lot, but there must be more in places we haven't looked yet." How are you going to know that you haven't overlooked something absolutely critical to understanding your issue, or that your information is up-to-date and comprehensive?

**When "Sufficient" Isn't Enough**

Some years ago, an individual student prepared a brief on the abortion issue for one of us. The student had found what he believed to be a sufficient amount of information on abortion, and set his entire analysis in the context of the question: should abortion be legalized? Unfortunately for the student's course grade, abortion *had* been legalized several years earlier by the Supreme Court in the *Roe* v. *Wade* decision. Incredible as it seems, the student had not talked about his information with the instructor (or presumably anyone else who was current on the issue) and asked: "What else is there to do?" Somehow he did not discover the Supreme Court's landmark decision or the resulting public controversy, a situation that made the student's analysis a tragicomedy. This is an extreme example to make a point: finding a significant amount of information on your topic is *not* in itself a guarantee that you have done adequate research. With an example as botched as the one just mentioned, there is no trouble locating what went wrong:

- ❑ Failure to discuss the issue brief with the instructor.
- ❑ Settling (presumably) for the first batch of documents found on the topic, possibly even the lazy fifth grader's encyclopedia report.
- ❑ Unsystematic or haphazard methods of research— in the example above, the student might just as well have stumbled across current material.

For most teams, knowing when they have met the conditions of doing thorough research is a bit more complicated and subjective, although they feel when they have done so. Great masses of material, however, don't ensure that you have met the thoroughness criteria. Here are some ways to judge whether your team has done a sound job of researching the literature on the topic. When you meet these conditions, it is time to turn to other forms of research:

1. *Sources Searched.* Have you looked up the topic in several places, such as the card catalog, various periodical indexes, other referencing and citation sources, and government documents? If you look only in the card catalog, you will miss entire groups of important documentary sources.

2. *Topics Explored.* Have you searched under related topic/subject headings? Not all of your information is likely to be found under one topic/subject heading; you must attempt to search related topics and to discover the other subject headings your topic is classified under. Occasionally, this opens up an entirely new vein of materials on the topic. Much of this new material will come from references in other documents you have found; there is a snowballing effect in research. Also, as a matter of good public relations, it lets your instructor know that you have made an honest effort to ferret out relevant information. Pay special attention to statistics; they change from year to year, and you want them to be as current as possible.

3. *Time Frame.* Has your search covered an appropriate period of time? Your team must decide the time periods to cover, but in most cases, the previous ten years is a good rule of thumb. It is essential to bring the topic fully up-to-date. This is usually done with such current sources as periodicals, newspapers, the Congressional Record, related documents on legislative activity, and interviewing stakeholders.

4. *Good Redundancy.* When you have met these three criteria, you will begin to experience the redundancy factor in research; you are turning up multiple citations of sources and finding very few, if any, new sources. When you have reached this point one of two interpretations is in order: your search has been thorough and is for all practical purposes complete, or you have completely missed a body of literature on your topic. Now that you know something about the range of reference materials available, you will have to decide which interpretation is correct.

## J.P. Student, Private Eye

If you have more or less followed our suggestions about doing research, you have been acting like detectives. You know that the search for information on a topic is not easy; you must work at finding what you want, and ask questions of yourself as you go. If frustrated in an effort, you have tried another path. Above all, you see that merely consulting references and card catalogs in a casual, uncritical fashion will not do; you know that you have to play an active intellectual role in researching the literature.

Therefore, Watson, if you approach research as a detective game, you will ask two focal questions: have we looked everywhere? and, have we looked logically? These are asked repeatedly during the research phase, serving as corrective guides. They are pivotal either when you feel you are having difficulty with your research efforts or when you begin to sense that you have completed them.

Treating research as detective work means expecting incompleteness, befuddlement, and confusion at times. You are tracing out a pattern, putting together a story, searching for leads, some of which are promising, some of which are dead ends. Above all else, you want your research to lay out a picture of who dunnit, and why did they? You are laboring on a jigsaw puzzle with its many little pieces to fit together; the interesting twist is that you are finding the pieces too— you are making your own puzzle as much as discovering one that is out there!

The more you can close the gap between what is out there and what you come up with, the better. In this regard your research activities should always have an analytical bent and should avoid the mere mindless collection of data. Why? Because as you gather data (information), if you stop to reflect on it as a potential piece of the puzzle, you give direction (where do we look now?) and coherence (what does this new evidence mean? how does it affect what we already know?) to your research.

The implications of research as detective work, therefore, are more than metaphorical, as the following example shows. Think of two teams researching a policy question. One team sends a member or two to the library to look up what's there on the topic, and then waits a couple of weeks to meet again to talk over what the two found. The other team talks about what they might find at the library and assigns each member a reference source (card catalog, government documents, newspapers, and so on) to cover for the next week's meeting. In this second team such things as standardized note taking, recording all references found, and what in general the team is looking for are discussed; the first team can't be bothered with such trivialities. Late in the term, the first team, is likely to visit the instructor to report: "There's not much on our topic," or, "We sent requests to some companies for information but haven't gotten anything back yet, so we haven't been able to do much. Now what should we do?" The question is whether you are going to take charge of the assignment, or let it drift aimlessly. Team number one is indifferent, insipid, and uninspired, and their product will be much the same; team number two is on the case and ready to make things happen, which they will.

Mystery cases do not solve themselves. The disappointments of research are a *constant* that can be expected. What your team does with and because of them is a *variable* under your control. Teams don't produce a successful issue brief with a passive, let-it-come-to-us style. Those who ferret out information and turn research into a game of whodunit have fun, learn something, and create excellent issue briefs.

## SLEUTHING THROUGH THE SOCIAL SCIENCE CITATION INDEX

Should your team be stuck or for any reason unsatisfied with its research efforts, you can do a very good job of tracing out your topic with an invaluable reference source, the *Social Science Citation Index*. At first glance the *SSCI* seems complicated and confusing, with its multiple volumes and directions sending the searcher from one volume to another to eventually find a complete reference. Do not be dismayed or put off by the *SSCI*. It is one of the best friends you have for tracing out streams of research, especially when you have fragmentary, partial leads. Here is a sketch of how it works; a little practice with it is all that is needed.

The *SSCI* is divided into four main indexing volumes called respectively, the *Citation Index, Corporate Index, Source Index,* and the *Permuterm Subject Index*. It fully catalogs 1,500 journals in the social, behavioral, and related sciences, including public and business policy, finance, and economics; and it also selects articles relevant to the social sciences from 3,000 other scientific journals, for a total of 4,500 journals that it covers. This alone makes it an attractive resource, but it is more than just a comprehensive catalog. The unusual feature of the *SSCI* is that it indexes *citations*, that is, it cross-lists the *references* that are used in all these journal articles.

The *SSCI* can be very helpful to the researcher because of the way it is organized. For example, you may start with a book (say Rachel Carson's famous book, *Silent Spring*) and ask: "Who has written about this particular work?" By knowing of Carson's book (either her name or the title will work) you can look in the *Citation Index* volume for a given year and learn the following: what other works Carson has written in that year, and what has been written about the book, or any other book or article she wrote in that year. That is, there is a listing of other authors and their relevant works who have cited Carson's book *Silent Spring* , or in addition, any other work she has done.

From here you have a choice of whether to go directly to the sources (that is, those other authors citing Carson) or to go on to the *Source Index* volume of the *SSCI*. The *Citation Index* volume gives abbreviated references (author's name, year, volume, page number) that direct you to books, journals, or reports that discuss Carson's work; that is one choice. The other path is to go to the *Source Index* volume for two things:   (1) a full reference of each of the works listed under Carson's book, and (2) a list of whose work the author is dealing with in the article or book for each reference found under Carson's name in the *Citation Index*. This information allows you to continue to trace out patterns and streams of research, that is, to discover what people are reading and writing about certain key works.

For instance, one article, found under Carson's heading in the *Citation Index*, dealt with the topic of "anti-science." When the author of the article was looked up in the Source Index, we learned that there were some other proponents of the so-called "anti-science" point of view, people such as Ralph Nader and Theodore Rozak. These names could then serve as key words or index terms to begin further searches. In this way you can use the *SSCI* to unearth new information for your topic or to check the thoroughness of what you have already found in other sources.

Using the *Citation Index* and *Source Index* allows you to tap into or discover bodies of research and literature you might otherwise not find.  It is time-consuming at first, but it is very rewarding and about as thorough as you can get. Additionally, some universities offer the *SSCI* in an electronic format, saving you the time of manual searching.

But this is not all the *SSCI* can do for you.  Imagine that you are told by a professor: "Say, I remember an article about gene splicing [your topic] a year or two ago; I think it was in *Science* and by a fellow named O'Hara . . . but then again, maybe it was the *AMA Journal* by a fellow named Ryan." How will you find this article if you are not certain about author, year, or title? You could go to the journal *Science* and look through it for those years; you could search for the author's name in one of several indexes; or you could search by subject (gene splicing) in any of several indexes.  If any of the information the professor gave you is correct, you should find the article eventually.  A much quicker way to handle partial or dubious references is to use the *SSCI Permuterm Index.*

The *Permuterm Index* can be used in the standard key-word subject search format or, and this is its main contribution, to ferret out sources with only partial knowledge of the words in the title.  This index is based on pairing significant words in the title (prepositions, conjunctions, and other insignificant words are omitted).  In this way you could find an article if you knew only one significant word in its title, or even if you had to guess at the words.  Additionally, it allows you to find related literature under one key-word subject and to get ideas about other subject headings to search under.

A risk of relying on this approach too heavily is that journal titles do not always contain key-word information about the contents.  Social science journals, for example, may have ponderous titles like *A Comparative Analysis of Multidimensional Human Resource Planning Considerations*, which you might have titled, *Personnel Planning in the U.S. and Great Britain.* Popular news magazines like *The Economist* are fond of using clever wordplay titles, like *Maggie Lays an Egg*, to describe Prime Minister Thatcher's failed efforts to reduce subsidization of the British poultry industry.

There is another volume of the *SSCI* that can expand your search or help you to find an incomplete source: the *Corporate Index.* Some reports, papers, and other materials are published not by individuals but by organizations, and they are rarely found in the card catalog.  This index is designed to let you look up an organization, say General Motors, to see what they have published on a topic. In addition, every five years *SSCI* prints a five-year cumulative index that contains an index of *Corporate/Subject* topics plus a geographical location section.

The geographical location of organizations section is helpful as follows. Say you want to know about something about nutrition in Poland. This index is just what you need. First you turn to the Poland section, and there you see that the Poland listings are subdivided by city. You would then read the listings of organizations in each city—which does not take long to skim—and see that there is a Food and Nutrition Institute in Warsaw. From this example you can see that the five year cumulative index will apprise you of organizations relevant to a wide variety of topics.

Assuming that you have searched the other sources cited in this chapter, if you search the *SSCI* in the manner suggested above and still have difficulty locating materials for your topic, then you are on firm ground in arguing that little relevant material exists on it. At this point you can argue that it is time to switch or radically alter your topic.

### GROUP DYNAMICS IN THE RESEARCH PHASE

With a team of five or six, it is common for each member to take on a portion of the research, with one or two perhaps doing the bulk of the research work. If your team values fairness in the allocation of chores, everyone *must* do a share of the research in some manner. As noted in earlier chapters, the team must decide what is a sensible and fair distribution of the workload, or disruptive and harmful group-dynamics problems may appear. Most of the teams we have seen share the research load more or less equally among members—a probable occurrence in American society and especially among college students who are skilled at looking out for their rights and interests. In some instances, typically because of the special expertise or preferences among team members, library research is done by only some of the members.

Perhaps one member does all the interviewing, while another collates and analyzes notes, generally acting as the team's executive secretary, while three members dig in and do the library research. We do not recommend this sort of division of labor as a first choice, since it may result in each person learning little that is new to them by avoiding unpleasant or difficult tasks they should be learning.  Nevertheless, we recognize that people tend to do what they are good at and to avoid what they are weak at; the team project, however, gives you the opportunity to improve your weak areas.

There is no shortage of work in the team, so as always, divide up the work fairly, that is, in a fashion that truly allows all members to feel that they are not exploited or exploiting.  A frequent pattern in teams is to evenly divide the preliminary research among all members, as in: "Joe, you search the card catalog for books and reference materials listed there; Mary, you search the periodical indexes; Horace and Anna, you search government documents; and I will search the newspaper indexes (for example, The *New York Times*, The *Washington Post*, The *Wall Street Journal* ).  We will meet next week to report on how much each has uncovered and then decide if we need to reassign ourselves, depending on what each of us finds." As you move on to more advanced stages of the research, you simply divide up work as the task requires.

We want to mention the *timing* of project stages as an important consideration in allocating tasks.  Imagine this:  your team is having its first or second meeting, and the workload is being divided.  You volunteer to direct the library research and do much of it yourself; others volunteer to do the analysis and put the paper together; others agree to be responsible for the class presentation.  Everyone feels that the division of labor is fair; everyone has taken on tasks they are willing to do.  Your research subteam finishes its preliminary search in two weeks, and in another four weeks the entire literature has been scanned.  You give your excellent and thorough notes to the analytical subteam and turn your attention to other classes or responsibilities.  This subteam, reasoning that it's only midterm and there's no rush, waits until after midterm exams to do anything.  Now there are five or six weeks left before the end of the term, and the presentation subteam is nagging the analytic folks for some material to work with.  You find yourself with more time to prepare for other classes, because your issue brief work was intense during the first half of the term, but you now have no issue brief duties; others are responsible.  Do you think your teammates will remember fondly the good work you did, the hard work you put in?  Quite the contrary; there are likely to be bitter accusations of laggard behavior on your part, now that the crisis is hitting and you're not doing anything anymore. You are going to be the bad guy. Never mind that they didn't do anything for the first seven weeks! Human memory is not necessarily just. The moral of this story is that it's better to allocate tasks smoothly across the entire term, and not divide the work totally in time-based units.

Teams that are fully engaged in the research tasks are likely to be humming like well-oiled engines. There may be some minor interpersonal or group dynamics difficulty, but it's nothing serious and isn't affecting the team's task accomplishments. If you are running smoothly, keep going. It is "merely" a matter of more sweat and thought from here to the finish.

Should your team be encountering time-consuming difficulties with the research, however, now is a critical period in which to save the project. Given all the work to do, a well-integrated team will spend most of its time on problems stemming from the assignment, things like: "How can we get this report from Chrysler in time? Should we call their corporate librarian and see if they'll fax a summary to us?" There may be personal disputes and dislikes among group members, but we have observed, and research has shown that these dislikes become of secondary importance or are simply forgotten about during the project. Well-integrated teams are busy at their projects and members do not care to get bogged down by questioning about why they dislike one another.

Weakly integrated teams, on the other hand, may be busy sniping at one another as in: "Boy, if *Elizabeth* would get off her duff, we might get somewhere with this thing! She's holding us up." In most instances, personal dislikes and bitter complaining are *symptoms*, not the *cause* of difficulty in getting the work done. Should your team be having problems either doing the research or with group dynamics, do not put them off any longer. Air out and resolve the problems, either as a team or with the assistance of the instructor or some neutral third party.

## CONCLUSION

A well-run team is having at least one meeting a week at this point and is beginning to make sense of all the information it has located. At these meetings the new information uncovered in the research is discussed, and perhaps the team will begin to spend time piecing it together in an attempt to analyze the issue as the team goes along. In other instances, teams merely discuss the evidence and do not push too far into analysis. It is desirable that the group should regularly spend a few minutes pondering how the evidence is fitting together and speculating on what it means. But what is really critical at this stage is that a comprehensive search is done and good notes are taken in preparation for the analysis that will follow.

## *ENDNOTES*

1. C. Wright Mills, *The Sociolocical Imagination* (Glencoe, IL: Free Press), 1959.
2. Audrey J. Roth, *The Research Paper* (Harford, CT: Wadsworth), 1982.
3. Matthew B. Miles and A. Michael Huberman, *Qualitative Data Analysis: A Sourcebook of New Methods* (Beverly Hills, CA: Sage Publications), 1984.

# 7

## TALKING IT OVER: RESEARCH WITH HUMAN SOURCES

For many researchers, a fascinating aspect of their work is the encounter with other human beings. For others, interviewing people is either unpleasant or seen as not terribly important, and is left to research assistants. In your team, interviewing may play an integral role, so we hope that you will enjoy it, or learn to do so.

Although it is trite to say it, the person best suited for gathering information from human sources is one who likes people. More to the point, it is the person who respects others and who is truly interested in learning what they have to say. Years ago, one of the authors was part of a research team interviewing elderly residents of a full-service elder hostel. One of our colleagues was especially concerned with maintaining professional distance from the interview subjects, and posed the prescribed questions in a flat voice, making little eye contact. Unfortunately, this style came across as bored or, worse, condescending, and she was verbally attacked by one subject who refused to give information to anyone so obviously uninterested in the trivial details of his life!

In this chapter you will learn how to find and talk with people who know something about your policy issue. These may include scholarly experts, journalists, participants in or witnesses to some event, government officials, corporate employees, advocates, or activists. The use of human sources plays an integral role, especially with topics that are relatively recent or where for some other reason little or incomplete accounts are written. For almost every policy case, contacting people who have a stake in the case, either as participants or observers, will illuminate and increase the interest of the issue brief. An interview with the right person can give you insights, leads, points of view, and information you might not get from written materials.

The interview process itself is uncomplicated. You identify people who may be able to tell you something you need to know, and you formally request an interview. You will ask your source a preplanned set of questions, and you will discuss any surprises that arise during the interview. The skills required for interviewing include setting your source at ease, asking good questions, and knowing how and when to end the interview. Above all, interviewing should be pleasant for you and the persons you interview. It is best thought of as a conversation where someone shares knowledge, experiences, and perhaps even wisdom with you— even though at times your subject may be hostile or tight-lipped.

## *WHOM SHOULD YOU INTERVIEW?*

From your library research, you will learn of people who have been active on the issue. Anyone who has commented on or is knowledgeable about the policy issue is a potential interviewee, and however you find them is really unimportant. As you learn who these observers or stakeholders are (that is, people with an interest in the policy who in some way are interested in its determination), your team may decide that interviewing some or all of them is vital to your project. Here are some reasons why you will interview people:

❑ There is little published information on the topic.
❑ It's a very new topic.
❑ Available information leaves too many questions unanswered.
❑ There are emotional or value-based dimensions to the issue that are never seen in print.

- ❑ The persons you want to interview have not published all of their findings.
- ❑ The persons are not likely to write about their experiences.
- ❑ You suspect that the real story is not being told in the media.

A good tactic is to interview a variety of observers and stakeholders with divergent viewpoints. In this way you can assemble a range of arguments and evidence for your team's consideration and analysis. A bad tactic is to assume that one speaker represents everyone in a paricular class or category. All steel makers do not have the same public policy interests; no factory worker can speak for every factory worker.

Once you have a list of persons to interview, the next thing to consider is what information you want from them. Many of these human resources readily accept an offer to be interviewed; a few are so busy that they may refuse or wish to avoid an interview. It is our experience that most busy people will give you some of their time— assuredly, a minority will not— or their staff's time, if you can present yourself convincingly in your initial contact with them. We return to how to be convincing below; for the moment we continue to consider what you need from them, and how they in turn respond to you.

There is a major choice you must make about the interview: are you looking for answers to specific questions that indicate you are familiar with the policy area? or are you a novice who is seeking the advice of an expert who can provide you with an overview of the policy area and homework that will make you more knowledgeable? You may fall somewhere in between these end points, but you must decide where you are on this continuum before you contact anyone for an interview, as the choice influences how you present yourself to them.

In most instances, it is best that you know all that you can before the interview contact is made, since some professionals will react by saying: "Why haven't you read my work on that?" (The interview is *not* appropriate as a quick way to avoid other research.) If you do not understand the author's works or are wondering about the implications of the author's views, then that is an appropriate interview topic. In some instances it is acceptable to interview in order to gain an overview of the area and to get better direction for your project, as long as you make it clear to the interviewee that this is what you are seeking. One of the worst things to do is to pretend knowledge to an expert, who will easily see how little you know. This type of "help me, I'm a dummy" interview is done when little published informa- tion is available, when you are having difficulty with your research, when you are critically short of time, or when the policy area is so massive or confusing that you need advice on how to think about and organize it. But be careful— do not use inter- views as a substitute for library research and the analysis that follows, use them in concert.

Everyone you interview has some particular stake or inter- est in the issue; otherwise they would not know much about it. While the degree and the amount of the stake varies greatly, it is useful for a *few* of those you interview to be considered neutral observers and commentators. The typical interviewee has a point of view and a bias to convey to you, so do not accept what they say without confirming or supporting it.

### CHOICES IN INTERVIEW STYLES: COVERAGE AND FORMAT

Once the subjects are chosen, an interview format must be designed. Now, two important questions face the interviewer: (1) how much relative weight should be given to breadth and depth of coverage of the issue? and (2) how much structure should be imposed on the questions asked?

### Coverage: Breadth and Depth

Let's look quickly at three types of interviews. An *item-specific interview* is a very focused question-and-answer session designed to give you some specific information that you need. An *information interview* is a general discussion with someone you believe to be knowledgeable on the subject and is designed to give you a broad overview of the subject, or possibly of your interviewee's knowledge of it. An *in-depth interview*, in contrast, is designed to let the interviewee share knowledge with you in more detail.

Item-specific and information interviewing may be as sim- ple as calling someone on the phone, explaining your project, and asking your question. If it really is that simple, don't try to make it more complicated by making an appointment, arranging to meet for lunch, or something equally time-consuming. Your interviewee will probably be glad to take five minutes to help you, but may be unwilling to take thirty minutes or an hour. Also, you risk damaging your credibility and that of your school or company when the interviewee discovers, if a longer interview is granted, that you asked for much more time than you needed.

If you really need more time and data than a quick phone call can provide, then longer information interviewing or even in-depth interviewing is required. Interviewing is a relatively costly activity; that is, a well-done interview takes time and energy to prepare, execute, and interpret. If you are asking for an hour or two of someone else's time, you should offer your own intelligent preparation in return.

### Format: More or Less Structured

In interviewing terms, structure has to do with the format in which you conduct the interview. You might think that an information interview is unstructured, while an in-depth interview is structured. In fact, there is no relationship between the type of interview and its structure. Interview structure depends much more on what you already know about the subject, and what you still want to find out.

An *unstructured interview* starts with a few broad, general questions, and then follows the flow of conversation wherever it leads. Use a free-flowing, adaptable, unstructured interview when:

- ❑  You aren't sure what the interviewee knows.
- ❑  You aren't sure what you should be asking. (This should happen because your topic is new and less visible, *not* because you are unprepared.)
- ❑  You want a broad overview of the interviewee's involvement with the subject.
- ❑  You want the interviewee to be comfortable enough to talk about sensitive subjects.
- ❑  You are not trying to confirm the same information among several interviewees.

A *structured interview* goes through a predetermined list of questions, and in its extreme form, for the sake of data reliability, requires that all informants be asked the same questions in precisely the same language. Use a structured interview when:

❏ You need answers to specific questions.
❏ You need to get answers on the same questions from different people.
❏ You want to confirm or validate information you have received from others.
❏ You are seeking a great deal of information and want to keep the interview moving so that everything is covered.

You can combine the two styles in a *semi-structured interview*. This format occurs when there are a number of specific or general questions that you must ask of everyone, and you are also willing to let the discussion flow as needed to get the information you want.

Further, in any interview style, it is often desirable to *probe* for more information. For example, you are asking several interest group representatives to answer the question: how does your membership support your lobbying efforts at the state level? Respondent *A* answers with a very specific list of behaviors that satisfy your knowledge needs. Respondent *B* answers: "Oh, they support it very well." You probe: "Could you tell me some of the ways they support your lobbying?" and the list is forthcoming. Respondent *C* answers: "Not too bad," and you probe as before. "Well," says *C*, "they seem to appreciate what we do for them." "That's good," you respond. "What in particular do they do to support you or help you?" And then *C* catches on and tells you what you wanted to know in the first place.

You can see that the type of interview will vary among your interviewees. Whichever types you use, your own preparation is the key to a successful interview.

## TELEPHONE OR IN-PERSON INTERVIEWS?

The next decision is whether to do *telephone* versus *in-person interviewing*. This choice may not exist when you want to talk with persons some distance from you, but if you are dealing with busy people in your own community, you will have this decision to make. To simplify things, we will go over the pros and cons of each type of interview. For information-gathering purposes, a well-done telephone interview should, in most cases, be as good as an in-person interview. Here is a brief comparison of in-person versus telephone interviewing. As you will see, they have much in common. So what should guide your choice?

Some people will express a preference on how they want to be interviewed. In these circumstances you must take what they offer, and wonder later if there is any significance to why they prefer one format over the other. Typically, if a telephone interview is preferred, it is because (a) respondents feel it will take less time, and/or (b) the respondents believe that they can maintain more control over the situation if the interviewer is not sitting there in the office.

You may prefer telephone interviews if you need to ask a few very specific, structured questions of many respondents. From your standpoint, the telephone interview is faster and cheaper, as you do not have to spend time and money to travel or to get dressed up to conduct it. In-person interviews can take quite a lot of your time, especially if each one is a great distance from another or if they must be done on different days. On the other hand, if you have opportunities to do in-person interviews with important persons, you may want to take them. You can observe where they work, their co-workers, their body language, and other nonverbal behaviors, and these observations may round out your interpretation of what you are told. Also, you may be able to read and respond to subtle cues of withholding, distress, hesitancy, and so on, thus getting more information from the respondents than they are initially willing to give.

Some researchers think that you can ask more personal, intimate, revealing, or soul-searching questions in person than you can over the telephone. If rapport is more easily established in person than over the telephone, so goes this reasoning, then you can ask about things you would not dare bring up on the telephone. In general this is correct, but for most policy briefs this need never arises. In addition, if your policy-related questions are too sensitive, the subject is likely not to answer them in person or on the phone. Finally, and in contrast to what has just been said above, there are occasions where the psychological distance and protection afforded by the telephone allows subjects to open up, like the persons pouring out their heartaches to the strangers next to them on planes. In such cases, the subjects know that you are a one-time contact who they never have to see at all, let alone again.

So the choice between telephone and in-person interviewing is primarily determined by: (a) the subjects' preference for one or the other, and (b) whether you feel it important to see persons at work in their surroundings, versus saving time and money by speaking with them on the telephone. Neither approach, in our experience, is in all circumstances superior to the other.


## MAKING CONTACT

When you have a list of people to interview, along with a set of questions to ask, you then want to know how to set up an interview, especially if you can say: "This is a very important person who'd never talk to us." Then, assuming an interview is granted, you'll have to get through it somehow, and get the information you need.

Our opinion is that most decisions about being interviewed are made in the initial telephone contact (a letter may precede the call), when the prospective subject sizes up the person requesting the interview. Here are guidelines for the telephone contact requesting an interview:

1. Prepare what you want to say and rehearse it, but try not to recite verbatim, as this will sound stiff and artificial over the phone.
   (a) Greet the person and immediately identify yourself and the university (or other organization) you are affiliated with; mention the name of anyone who has referred you or any other connection that might be of aid in getting the subject to talk to you.
   (b) State your business. For example: "I know that you are an expert in nuclear waste disposal, and my team is working in the policy area of toxic waste legislation. Could we please interview you for our project?"
   (c) Be alert for unexpected reactions by the subject that may force you to alter your prepared remarks; that is, be nimble and flexible if the subject throws you a curve. For example, if the person responds to your greeting by saying: "I'm due at a meeting in two minutes," you must instantly judge the situation. Say either: "I'll call you back. When would be a good time?" or, "Briefly, I'm doing a project on X and would very much like to talk with you about it."

**2.** Don't act. Avoid talking in a tone that is too familiar or personal (as in the "gee, it's s-o-o-o nice to talk to you" effusive style, or as if you've known the subject for years). On the other hand, don't be too formal and pompous (trying to sound like a deep-voiced, serious professional). What you should sound like is an attentive student who is seeking the insight of a more experienced person.

**3.** Be prepared to answer specific questions, but do not raise them on your own before you get a commitment to the interview. The subject may inquire: "How long is this going to take?" "Are you coming to my office or can we do this over the phone?" "Are you sure you want to talk to me? Why?" "I'm busy for the next two weeks, can you wait that long or would you rather talk to my assistant?", "Tell me more about your project. . ." and, "Is what I say to you held in confidence or is it for the public record?" Try to anticipate these kinds of questions and have answers ready; the last thing you want is fumbled answers to questions; they harm your chances of getting the interview.

**4.** Be prepared to negotiate. If subjects hesitate or say no, do not give up without a courteous counteroffer. Try such gentle tactics as: "We really do want to talk to you, is there any time we could arrange it at your convenience? Your views are critical to our analysis; is there any way you could squeeze us into your schedule?" or, "We can wait a few weeks, if your schedule is that tight." As a last option, try: "May we submit a few written questions to you, and could you answer them in writing or on a tape we will provide?"

    (a) If you cannot get anywhere negotiating, there is no need to push hard, as a hostile interview is undesirable in these circumstances. Instead, try to get a few questions in over the phone as you are being turned down, for example: "O.K. Mr. Jones, you do sound terribly busy and thanks anyway; perhaps right now could you tell us who else we might try to interview? Could you tell us where to look for more information and people to interview in the industry? Could we ask just a couple of quick questions now? Is it accurate that your position is that all or most nuclear reactors are comparatively safe to operate?"

    (b) Be alert for the possibility that subjects may change their minds and agree to be interviewed after all, or that they may give you time *then and there* for a short interview.

    (c) If the subject expresses anxiety or distrust about being quoted or in any way identified in your issue brief, you will have to negotiate the confidentiality issue on the spot (see below).

**5.** Have paper, pencil, and calendar at hand to write down times when interviewing is possible, answers to questions, and other important information. It seems obvious, but respondents will not be happy about talking to an interviewer who says: "Uh, wait a minute, I've gotta find a pencil."

6. Once granted an interview, find out how much time you have to conduct it. Ask for what you think you will need, but be advised that most subjects will not give more than an hour and some will only give you 15 to 20 minutes. If you need more time and can schedule a series of interviews, do so. You will want to set them up only after the first interview is completed, thereby allowing you to judge the subject and for the subject to judge you.

Almost without fail, a potential interviewee asks before agreeing to be interviewed: "So, what do these people need to know from me? Are they going to waste my time, or are they worth it?" Thus, it is in the first contact that you must present yourself in a manner that makes your case. What you have going for you is established professionals' normal willingness to help students; if you can come across as sincere, intelligent (which is not the same as well-informed), and interested in them and their work, you will probably get interviews, providing they have no overriding reasons for not granting them. Finally, above all, try to relax when making the contact call. The odds are in your favor that the person will want to help you and is flattered that you would call for an interview.

## THREE P's OF INTERVIEWING

Whatever the mode and format of interviewing you choose, your prime tasks are to be prepared, polite, and pointed. You have asked another person to give you something valuable— a piece of his or her time. Make the most of it, and respect the gift!

**Be prepared.** If you are planning to tape the interview, have the equipment ready and *be sure that you have asked the subject's permission to tape*; by professional research standards it is unethical to tape without the subject's consent. Your questions may be structured— very specific and precisely worded— and you may even give the subject a set of responses to make, such as "strongly agree" to "strongly disagree." Or the questions may be open-ended— meant to probe for memories and views instead of having a prescribed set of responses to choose from.  There is no prohibition, of course, against combining the two techniques.  Your research on the topic will guide you in the construction of the interview questions.

Do not depend on your memory.  Write down everything you want to ask during the interview and, moreover, do this well before the interview so that you have ample time to reflect on your questions and alter them as needed.  One of the misguided acts we have seen students perform is to rush to conduct an interview without leaving time to ponder it and perhaps change it.  Afterwards, their lament is: "I can't believe I didn't ask him . . ." or, "Boy, those questions weren't well thought out."

Being prepared also means having several pens or pencils and paper on hand, and any notes, articles, books, or whatever that you might want to read from or refer to in the interview.  Finally, being prepared means having a watch or clock handy and having an idea of how long the interview will last so that you can ask the most important questions first and save the less vital ones for later, where they can be omitted or quickly covered if time runs short.  Since people will take different amounts of time to respond to the same question, it is difficult to know how long the interview will take.  Nevertheless, the subject almost always places a limit on how much time you will have, normally anywhere from 15 minutes to an hour.  So be prepared to amend or sacrifice questions if your time is running short.

***Be polite.***  There is little to say here, other than to remind you that your orientation is that the interviewee is doing you a favor.  Avoid cancelling interviews or making last-minute changes in them; be prompt about appointed times; even if you are treated rudely, hang in there to try to get the information you want.  Only if you are truly insulted and poorly treated should you protest— with professional decorum— to the subject; you want what the subject has and as the saying goes, you catch more bees with honey than with vinegar.

Some interviewees have a seemingly endless answer for each question and this talkativeness must be curbed without insult.  Should you have a talkative subject, do not simply give in and let the subject ramble on and on, because your time will be wasted if you do.  You need to interrupt the subject ever so gently by saying something like: "That's fascinating and it leads me to my next question. . . " or, "Your elaboration is very helpful and I'd like to return to it after we get the basics down on the questions I have prepared for the interview" or, "Wow, I didn't know that; can we come back to that later?"

**Be pointed.** Use your time and that of the subject's as efficiently and effectively as possible within the context of politeness. (A fast way to end an interview is to give the subject the feeling that you are rushing through the interview or making unfair demands.) Keep in mind that many professionals purposefully have the secretary interrupt with a telephone message a few minutes into the interview. This is a face-saving (though cowardly!) technique for ending an interview, as the subject says: "Oh, sorry, something urgent has come up and we'll have to stop talking sooner than we had planned."

We have already told you to know what you want from the subjects and to get to it as soon as they allow. Still, though, single-minded efficiency can backfire with your subjects. Some want to be warmed up with a little idle chatter, and if rushed they clam up because they feel exploited or pushed around. Some are all business and go right into a mode that indicates: what can I do for you while you are using my precious time? With these people, get right to it. Most, however, want to chat for a few minutes (either at the beginning or end or even in your first contact where you request the interview) about you and themselves. This is a good sign, so let it happen. At some point the getting-acquainted chatter stops and it's up to you to sense when. Now you must switch to asking your questions. In other words, do not go on with stories that may bore the subject. When the subject stops talking, or only responds to what you say with "Oh," "Ah, hah," "I see," "yeah," it is probably time for the real interview to begin.

### IN-PERSON INTERVIEWING

Now we turn to the specifics of in-person interviewing. What counts most here is your awareness that you are putting all of yourself— it is not just an oral performance as on the telephone— on display for the subject. Your facial expressions, how you dress, speak, and carry your body will make an impression; it is hard to follow this with the invocation to be relaxed in the interview, but that is precisely what you need to do. Keep in mind that the subject wants to help you and is probably a little nervous too. Being relaxed, or being able to relax once the interview commences, is your first task.

In terms of appearance, consider how the subject sees you. In almost all instances you should dress in professional attire—that ordinarily means a suit or sport coat and tie for men, and a suit or dress for women. However, it is good to learn something about the subjects and what they might expect you to look like. In some rare cases professional dress is the wrong uniform, as indicated by what a coal miner in one of our classes said: "When they [corporate executives] come out here to see us in their Brooks Brothers suits, we know they really don't know what we're all about." The general rule is to dress professionally unless you have reason to change your dress to fit in with those you are interviewing. A caveat is needed here; do not attempt to fit in if you suspect that in doing so you will appear silly, phony, or out of character in any disrupting manner. And it's generally better to be just a bit underdressed than the reverse. That is, a sport coat and tie will get you by in a business suit environment, but a business suit in the coal mine is definitely overdressed!

Who will do the interviewing in your team? A team member with interview experience seems a sound choice, but don't overlook the desire of team members to learn a new skill. In such a case use two members, the experienced one and the novice, for interviews. If no team member has done interviewing, what can you do? The answer is to practice with each other or to consult your instructor for guidance.

Here are a few suggestions for practice interviews. First, think of this practice as a role-playing exercise where the roles of subject and interviewer are taken seriously. That is, make the practice as real as possible, since this adds significantly to the learning of the participants. You need a room with a chair and desk where the subject will sit, and a chair in front of it, where the interviewer will sit. Both subject and interviewer should dress for the part, and go through the routine of knocking on the door at the appointed time, and so on. Make it seem as real as possible and do not lapse into giggling or hammed-up asides that break the focus of the role playing.  If you do this, you will have several gains: identifying bugs or awkwardness in the questions, learning how to ask questions and deal with the dynamic interchanges of interviewing, and very importantly, getting used to the role of interviewer.  (Some of our students have even used such practice sessions to get used to wearing their business clothes without twitching, tugging, and looking desperately uncomfortable!)

### *NOTES AND TAPES: RECORDING INFORMATION*

Now consider the matters of note taking and taping interviews. We advise that you always take notes either in the interview or as soon afterwards as possible, whether or not you are also taping.  The decision about note taking or taping (you can of course do both) involves what taping will do to help or hinder you.   There is no definitive answer to the question of the superiority of taping versus note taking; each has its benefits and drawbacks.  As a rule, we suggest that note taking without taping be your normal mode of operation; it is best to take good notes and to use the tape recorder only when it is mandatory.

Why do we take this position? First, it is good experience for you to take notes without the aid of a tape recorder.  Note taking makes you think and organize more as you go, and it keeps your attention focused on what the subject is saying.  Second, if you tape, there is the requirement to listen to the tapes again and then to take written notes; that is, you can't use a tape recorder as a substitute for note taking because you'll still have to take notes. On occasion, you will find that you want to stop taking notes and just focus in on what the subject is telling you; that is fine now and then, but do not make it a common practice.

Three situations in which taping is advised, assuming the subject has given permission to be taped, are: (1) when a complicated story is being told and you want to get all the details and nuances correct; (2) when the subject is reciting statistical or other such material that requires attention to details for accuracy (in many instances, however, the subject can give you hard copy for this purpose); and (3) when you have reason to believe that you will need to return to the verbatim interview, perhaps to compare interviews or to quote accurately.

Beyond these considerations, you must make a judgment as to whether a tape recorder will inhibit the subject. Our experience is that it normally does not. If a sensitive issue comes up on which the subject does not want to be on the record,the subject can request that the tape be turned off while a confidential account is given. You are obliged, by rules of professional ethics, to respect such confidences.

### CONFIDENTIALITY AND ANONYMITY

This brings us to the subjects of confidentiality and anonymity. A *confidential* interview means that the subject's remarks (some or all of them, according to the terms negotiated) will not be attributed to the subject directly or in a fashion so that would indentify the source. That is, confidentiality means the subject is not identified by name, and it further means that statements which could be used for identification will be omitted or suitably disguised—without distorting them in any critical way—from your issue brief. Therefore, to promise that a subject's statements are confidential is to guarantee that only the interviewer, and presumably the rest of the team, know who gave the interview. Confidentiality is a topic for negotiation. It is inadvisable to offer it at first unless the subject raises questions about it. If confidentiality is important you can make it a bargaining point if the subject uses it as an excuse for not granting the interview: "Oh, I see, Dr. Caruthers. Well, I can assure you that the interview will be confidential." You can also negotiate limited confidentiality, letting the subject know exactly how you intend to use quotes or the interview in your report, or giving review privileges over the portions of the report that he is quoted.

If the subject agrees to be interviewed under the condition that it is a confidential interview, then you have waived your right to quote and paraphrase in such a manner as to identify the subject or the subject's organization. You are professionally obligated to respect your promise and the subject's privacy.

Anonymity, in contrast, means that even the researchers do not know who each individual subject is. An example of anonymity is mailing out questionnaires to subjects without any identifying codes or markings on them, thereby making each subject's identity unknown to the researchers. We bring this point up, since some researchers think it useful to place codes on questionnaires so that they will know to whom to send a second mailing of the questionnaire. This is efficient, but it requires some special procedures if the subject's anonymity is to be preserved. In issue brief interviewing, confidentiality comes up regularly and anonymity rarely, since obviously one cannot conduct an interview as if in a priest's confessional.

## *CONCLUSION*

Research with human subjects is distinctly different from library research. Books, periodicals, abstracts, and documents do not react to you or have sensitivities that require your considered attention. When dealing with people who are potential subjects, remember that they are initially asking themselves questions like: "What do they want from me?" "Can I trust them?" "Are they worth the effort and time required on my part?" "How can I persuade them that my point of view is accurate?" Do not let these questions frighten or intimidate you, for a forthright, down-to-earth approach to your subjects is all they are looking for. Almost all of those you contact will want to help you in some way, and it is your job to allow them to do so.

In addition to being honest with human sources, which conveys your respect for them as people rather than as pieces of data, you will additionally show your respect by being prepared to talk with them in the initial contact and in the interview. Your confidence and calmness are boosted and your anxiety is reduced when you are well prepared for contact with human sources. With just a little effort and attention, this should be a most enjoyable part of the project for your team.

As with library and other documentary research, talking with people will contribute to the continuous process of gathering and analyzing information. In the next chapter we move directly into the closing of the circle, as research comes to an end and the analysis of all the data and materials you have examined begins.

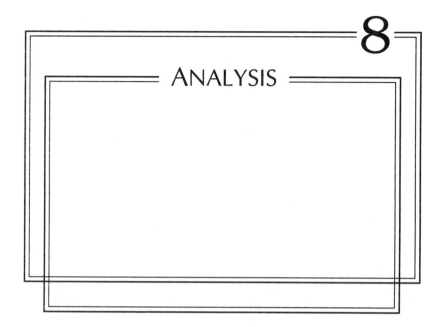

# 8

## ANALYSIS

When you begin to find little or no new evidence, you have done enough research. Three questions you have been pondering now come into prominence: (1) what does all this mean? or, more operationally, how do we do our analysis? (2) how do we reach and support our arguments and create the policy recommendations (conclusions) that flow from them? and finally, (3) what is the best (simplest yet sophisticated and effective) way to present our findings?

In this chapter we go into depth on the first two questions, saving the last question for upcoming chapters on writing and orally presenting the issue brief.

It is in this stage of analysis that a major advantage of the issue brief format comes into prominence. Whether doing a strategic-management issue brief or a public-policy issue brief, the framework is at hand to guide your organization and presentation, in writing and orally. You can follow a ready-made outline and forget the difficulty often involved in deciding how best to organize and present your work.

Thus far in the project, your efforts *primarily* have been to gather information, and only *secondarily* to assess it. Information gathering inevitably leads to its assessment, even if you don't really mean to be analyzing at the time. As a result, your

team, especially if you have steadily discussed your research
efforts at meetings, will arrive at the analysis stage with alternatives, scenarios, hypotheses, and hunches about the policy
problem's scope and possible solutions. Now, though, you will
do a more formal analysis suitable for presentation in the issue
brief.

## A DILEMMA: REACHING CLOSURE
## AND ENCOURAGING IDEAS

There are balancing acts here, not surprisingly. On the one
hand, time is running out and you need to reach closure on the
issue. This means that team consensus is needed on various
dimensions of the topic and how to analyze it. On the other
hand, you want to take advantage of the skills, viewpoints, and
creative potential in the team, which means that you do not want
to close off consideration of alternatives (both ideas and methods
of analysis), no matter how harebrained, impossible or irrelevant
they seem. So, to reach closure and consensus, you hear out
your teammates as they talk about ideas and analytical paths,
and establish shared rules about evaluating and disposing of
those ideas.

If your team has built up a good sense of trust, morale, and
communication, you can encourage one another to take the risk
of expressing ideas without fear of ridicule, rejection, and hu-
miliation. We have seen repeatedly in groups that it is not
merely intellectual ability that produces a high-quality issue
brief; it results equally from the group cohesion which engenders
support and good ideas among members. The best work we have
seen is from teams where members do not feel inhibited about
expressing their ideas to one another. And some of the weakest
issue briefs we have encountered are from teams with very
intelligent individuals where dissent was not tolerated, and
reaching closure in accord with the views of one or two dominant
members was the inevitable end.

Here's a way to move toward closure without shutting off
free expression in the team. Use a flip chart or chalkboard to
record ideas as are they expressed. Establish the rule that
during a free-flowing idea session, criticism or any sort of
feedback on ideas is not permitted. As each idea is stated, write

it down. When it is clear that the flow of ideas has stopped, then the team can go back to the list and systematically evaluate each idea. The first step is to group those ideas that are alike. The second step is to apply some relevant criteria to the remaining few ideas. Criteria might include some of the following:

1. The idea will not cost an unreasonable amount of time or money to implement.
2. The idea can actually be implemented by the team.
3. The idea is directly relevant to our topic; it is not an interesting sidetrack.
4. The idea clarifies some things that have been puzzling us.
5. The idea will give us a competitive edge over teams that have been less creative.

### BALANCING CONVERGENCE AND DIVERGENCE

A good way to converge on the problem—and of course to see how divergent your views are—is to have a session devoted to each member's conception of its scope and solution(s). It is best to have each member write out a short essay or outline and present it to the group. Writing is thinking, and for most people, having to put it on paper is of immense aid to understanding and refining what they know. You should do this even if the team has rigidly divided the tasks so that each member has worked only on a portion of the issue to this point.

When you hear teammates' views, ask questions: do you agree? are your differences substantive or semantic, that is, are you arguing over real content or over a choice of words? had you thought of that yourself? does what they say fit with or can it be made to fit with, your views? The definition of the problem determines the way the team will analyze it, and even though you arrived at a definition of the problem in an earlier phase, you now appreciate that it is a working, dynamic definition, subject to alteration in light of new thoughts and evidence.

Given the composition of the group and the topic, your team may not encounter difficulty converging on the problem. Instead, some teams have few differences and agree on how the topic is assessed and handled during the problem-definition phase. This allows them to consensually modify it as they do research.  Then when they reach the analysis phase they agree on what the problem is and how to deal with it.  If this describes your team, congratulations!  But now ask yourselves:  Is it because you have worked as a team and thought hard and considered alternatives, or has the team overlooked or avoided aspects of the topic?  Beware of groupthink, where false closure is reached because much evidence has been omitted or ignored because of group dynamics that impose conformity of thought as the price of acceptance.  Groupthink is a possibility in any group, especially one where one or two members assume intellectual and psychological dominance.

Any divergent views on the analysis should be seriously considered and resolved in such a way that all members are satisfied that they are not being cajoled or ignored.  Should your team still be divided at this point, you should consider the option of having members prepare minority reports (discussed later).  Furthermore, recall that as part of the issue brief format you are required to take the viewpoint of a stakeholder, a person or group interested in the policy, with whom you do not necessarily agree, and this perspective may solve the dispute.  Much of the analytic work can still be done as a group effort and this safety valve of the minority report separates those who disagree out of conviction from those who are inclined to be critical without backing up their sentiment with effort.


## APPRECIATING DIFFERENCES
## IN LEARNING/THINKING STYLES

Even though we portray a near worst case scenario above, our experience is that the vast majority of teams have no major difficulty agreeing among themselves at this phase of the issue brief.  Yet some teams do encounter friction at this stage when individual members see that the way they think is not the way everyone else thinks.

Consider how differences in the thinking styles of team members can affect the team.  Some teams produce excellent issue briefs as a result of, and not despite, intense argument and critical appraisal of their diverse ideas and approaches.  If serious differences or conflicts surface, these can be honest differences rooted in how people think.  Differences in styles of thinking and problem solving can be a formidable burden on the team or, with a little effort, a source of a thorough and creative issue brief.

Some people may be unsettled or downright anxious to find out at this stage that they have sharply differing opinions on the topic. For example, the topic's complexity, novelty, ambiguity, and uncertainty may be seen in a starkly different fashion, as when one member sees a clear and simple solution, while another has unanswered and troubling questions. Imagine a team where the members find out that their views of the topic and procedures for analyzing it are not in accord. A common reaction is a defensive one: "Boy, Jim is so (pick your label) stubborn, stupid, naive, lost. . . Why does he go on like that? He's got it all wrong. Why can't he see what I'm talking about?" Jim, of course, may be having similar thoughts about his teammates.

We suggest to teams whose members are confused or in conflict— because members do not agree on how to do the analysis and define the problem— to ask themselves if differences in thinking style are involved. A useful tool is Kolb's Learning Style Inventory,[1] which divides the way people learn, their thinking/problem solving styles, into four types by the intersection of two polar dimensions, as illustrated in Figure 8.1. This way of thinking about thinking has helped many students and professionals to better understand themselves and their teammates by making them aware of and taking advantage of their differences. It is also a good tool for conflict resolution or accommodation of others' views.

Just what do we mean by learning/thinking style? We illustrate this below with Kolb's model. Each of the four thinking styles has its strengths in various aspects of problem solving. This phenomenon goes by several labels: right brain versus left brain thinking, intuition versus logic (or verbal symbolization), hard versus soft, scientific versus artistic, analytic versus synthetic. Precisely what you term it is not important as long as you understand that if channeled properly, a team comprised of members with contrasting styles of thinking and problem solving is at an advantage.

1. *Execution (concrete and active).* This kind of activity is required to advocate positions or ideas, set objectives, commit to schedules, commit resources, and implement decisions.

┌─**FIGURE 8.1  Kolb's Learning Model\***────────────────────────────────┐

CONCRETE EXPERIENCE

| | |
|---|---|
| *Execution\** | *Divergence* |
| Strength: | Strength: |
| Accomplishment | Generation of |
| Goal-oriented | alternatives |
| action | Creativity |

ACTIVE ─────────────────────────┼───────────────────── REFLECTIVE
EXPERIMENTATION                                                    OBSERVATION

| | |
|---|---|
| *Convergence* | *Assimilation* |
| Strength: | Strength: |
| Focusing efforts | Planning |
| Decision making | Formulating |
| | theory |

ABSTRACT CONCEPTUALIZATION

\*Execution is suggested to replace Kolb's original term, Accomodation, by Carlson, Kean, and Martin.[2]
*Source:* Adapted from Kolb, 1984

└──────────────────────────────────────────────────────────────────┘

2. *Divergence (concrete and reflective).* This kind of activity is required to seek background information and to sense opportunities, investigate new patterns, recognize discrepancies and problems, and generate alternatives.
3. *Convergence (abstract and active).* This kind of activity is required to select among alternatives, focus efforts, evaluate plans and programs, test hypotheses, and make decisions.
4. *Assimilation (abstract and reflective).* This kind of activity is required to develop theory, compare alternatives, establish criteria, formulate plans and hypotheses, and define problems.

Ideally, the team with each of these styles represented does—other things being equal—a truly terrific issue brief. If your team is having trouble that could be attributed to different thinking/learning styles, by taking the Kolb Learning Style Inventory and discussing it you may realize that your "rigid," "strange," or "dull" teammates have a method to their madness. Moreover, you may see that you are entrenched in one style that conflicts with other styles present in the group. For example, convergers and divergers frequently pull the team in opposite directions, as do assimilators and executors. Thinking styles can have different effects at different stages of the issue brief process, as we see here:

1. *Executors* are the ones who keep saying: "Let's get this done!" When the team spirit is lagging, this is often just what's needed. When the final product must be readied, the executor keeps things moving. But this type must be careful not to push too fast and too far, forcing hasty and poorly thought out decisions about how things should be done.

2. *Divergers* like to come up with creative insights and new ideas, but are reluctant to settle on how the problem is going to be defined, or to fully think it through and plan how it can be analyzed. Clearly, then, the divergers can play a vital role, but they must realize that some bounds, schedules, and plans must be agreed upon to make progress.

3. *Convergers* are able to put ideas together in packages, bringing diverse opinions closer to consensus. This is a wonderful skill in an argumentative group, and is especially valuable as the project draws near to a close. Convergers may seek consensus too early, however, and thus freeze out good ideas that are never spoken.

4. *Assimilators* are the strategic planners and theorists of the group. Their skills are especially useful in the beginning, when tasks must be identified and allocated, and during analysis, when sense must be made of the mountain of evidence. They may be impatient with the details of researching, recording, sorting, and writing, instead preferring to focus on the big picture.

Style of thinking is not the only dimension that can divide members. Political views, a psychological need to dominate or submit, experience with the topic, specific feelings aroused by the topic, and so on may also play a role in shaping how a member wants to deal with the issue. The best way to cope with such matters is to talk them through and search for the common ground we discussed in the earlier section on conflict resolution.

## TOOLS OF ANALYSIS

We use the term *analysis* in its broadest sense to connote the total intellectual scrutiny of the policy issue. Your guiding questions are of two basic types. The first concerns questions that critically examine the components of an argument, such as: how does this work? how do the parts work together? The second kind of question focuses on: what if? what might be? and, how can things be fitted together in a new manner? That is, these questions involve the ability to imagine how seemingly unrelated evidence and concepts that go into supporting an argument might be combined to form a new explanatory whole. We now deal with each type of question and the methods you can employ to answer them.

**Sorting the Pieces**

Your team is likely to have a mountain of reports, articles, books, interview notes, and so forth that have been collected and cursorily inspected or outlined. Now you want to gain a deeper understanding of the arguments, the premises, and conclusions in those documents. On the basis of this understanding, you will evaluate the arguments to find their strengths and deficiencies. Once this is done, you can then arrive at your own conclusions and propose creative solutions about society's or the organization's best interests. Then, for the public-policy issue brief, you will take the perspective of a stakeholder group and argue their case; and for the strategic-management issue brief you will put together an opposing point of view and scenario of the company's best interests.

As a first step, you must decide how to handle the vast amount of information you have collected. One thing you should not do is succumb to the psychological temptation to throw out or give scant attention to much of what you have collected. Sifting, sorting, and prioritizing will allow you to manage your information. The desire to jettison information is strong because human beings have a need to reduce uncertainty and they are psychologically inclined to place limitations on the amount of information they attempt to comprehend in a short period of time. Hence a common response to this information overload is to focus on a few sources of information while ignoring the rest. Also, a mountain of data (notes, copies, interview tapes) provides a rich opportunity for the procrastinators among you to say: "I'll do it tomorrow." As with any large task, you overcome this problem by dealing with the data one piece at a time.

You will need some sorting rules to guide you in this process and to prevent you from overlooking important items while enabling you to handle a large amount of information. We assume that you simply do not have the time to fully analyze every document you find in your research. Indeed, your team has no doubt already excluded some material as irrelevant or tangential during the research-gathering phase.

At a minimum, you must thoroughly read some documents and speed or skim read every document you have. Skimming takes place first, so you can get a sense of what each document is about. Once this is accomplished, try to sort your materials by category:

- ❑ By stakeholders' viewpoints.
- ❑ By the nature of conclusions or solutions proposed.
- ❑ By supporting and opposing views on some key point.
- ❑ By the time sequence in which events occurred and documents appeared.
- ❑ By any other category that lets you reduce the complexity and make more sense.

Are there two, three, four or more stakeholders or policy recommendations involved in the issue? Can you differentiate them from one another so that you have stakeholder groups *A, B, C,* and so on? Can you identify two or three clear positions on the issue and categorize data in that way? Will a chronology help you organize the information and understand it better?

As a second sorting technique, try to assess the quality of your documents. For more intensive examination, select those texts that appear to state the positions of stakeholders' arguments in the most thorough and convincing manner. (This assumes, of course, that when you skimmed all the documents, you did not overlook vital portions of their contents!) If you can divide your materials into stakeholder groups— or similar arguments of several stakeholders— who support differing policies, this will allow you to reduce a massive stack of materials into several smaller stacks of logically related and cognitively manageable documents. As noted above, should you have a better method, use it, as long as you attain the goal of sorting, without overlooking important evidence, to reduce the mass and complexity of the materials you have gathered.

   With this done you are ready to assess the documents chosen as focal, and then to use the results as a model to return to the other documents for a final inspection and evaluation. Evaluating the argument(s) in a text is demanding and time-consuming work, yet its rewards can be exhilarating. You will experience this when you sigh: "Whew, I finally see what this guy is up to and how it is connected to the rest of the information we have."


## *EVALUATING ARGUMENTS*

Sometimes arguments are presented in a clear, logical, and deductive style, and it is quite easy to locate the premises and conclusions— although this does not mean that you automatically will understand them. Unfortunately, this type of text is not always the one you will find, nor is it always the best kind of argument to make. Some arguments, for instance, are presented metaphorically, analogically, or allegorically. Some do not rest on established factual premises but rather on inferences that might be correct, or on creative insight where proof is difficult to articulate or find. Further, a text may contain subarguments in addition to the main argument. And, of course, some arguments are convoluted, complex, purposefully or unconsciously deceptive, or merely poorly made. Moreover, some arguments are not based upon reason and proof, but on assertion without proof, attacks on others, appeals to the reader's biases, and arguments based solely on authority.

   For some sound and easily followed methods of critically outlining and evaluating arguments, as well as distinguishing the ones based on logic and reason from others, see Boylan's *The Process of Argument;* and for a more formal and thorough approach, see Fisher's *The Logic of Real Arguments.*[3] For a complementary set of analytic techniques focused on problem solving, see Lewis and Greene's *Thinking Better.*[4] (And as suggested earlier, browse through adjacent call numbers to find other books of help to you on the topic of logic and argumentation.) Here we can relay some of Boylan's suggestions and also introduce a second tool of argument evaluation, Toulmin's warrants, claims, backing model.[5]

Boylan suggests that a logical outline, which is not a mere *classification* of the contents but a *logical summary* of the argument, should be prepared for those texts that you have decided are central to your analysis. He says that devoting great effort to outlining critical texts is a key to organizing and understanding the arguments and conclusions in other materials you cannot devote as much time to assessing. After gaining comprehension of the arguments of a few central documents, you then should be able to locate and assess the arguments in those documents you will skim.

As Boylan instructs, the more common difficulties in analyzing an argument are those of *finding* and then *distinguishing* premises from conclusions.[6] The degree of difficulty will vary with each text you analyze. Here are some helpful techniques. The first task is to identify the document's thematic context. You do this by asking: why did the author write this? overall, what is the author trying to tell the reader? what's the point of writing this? If this does not work, says Boylan, pretend you are either a newspaper reporter in search of a summarizing headline or a lawyer seeking the essence of your opponent's case. This puts you into a frame of mind concentrated on identifying conclusions and premises. First you find the conclusion, what the author wants to convince the reader of, and then you go back to seek the premises by asking: what does the author offer as support for this conclusion? If you have difficulty locating the conclusion, Boylan suggests you look for key words and phrases which usually indicate a *conclusion*:

> . . . therefore, hence, thus, consequently, so, it follows that, it must be that, we may infer that, necessarily, now we can see that, it is now evident that, shows that, indicates that, proves that, entails that, implies that, establishes that, or allows us to believe that.[7]

That done, you may be able to find the *premise(s)* as a part of the thematic context. If you cannot locate them in this way here are key words to look for:

> because, so*, since, in order to, for the reason that, for, assuming that, is shown by, is indicated by, is proven by, is entailed by, is implied by, is established by, in that, due to the fact that, given that, may be concluded from, inasmuch as.[8]

*[NOTE: Depending on the context, so can signal either a conclu-
sion or a premise; so, be alert when you encounter it!]

Another technique that may help in analyzing arguments
involves searching out, as you learned to do earlier, any reviews,
letters, debates, and so forth generated by the document under
analysis. Using the techniques for finding such commentaries
may reward you with a whole or partial analysis of the document.
This is not to say that you accept the commentary on its face.
It too is subject to analysis. But such commentary is often a
source of ideas or added perspectives for teams.

A word on suppressed premises— premises that for one
reason or another are not explicitly stated in the argument yet
are assumed to be understood by the reader— is in order. They
are important because they are common and ask the reader to
fill in an inferential gap in the argument, and as such can be
deceptive or confusing. An example Boylan offers of a suppressed premise is a campaign slogan: Experience Counts; Vote
John Doe.[9] For convenience and because it is obvious, the
premise that *John Doe has experience* is omitted, even though
the argument is incomplete without it. The additional premise
that John Doe has *relevant* experience is also to be inferred,
though it is unstated and unsupported. Building on Boylan,
here are three criteria we suggest for accepting suppressed
premises:[10]

1. Does it fill in an inferential gap or is it an unsupported inference
   in itself? (which may invalidate the conclusion).
2. Does it support the general tenor and direction of the argument?
3. Does it contradict any other position of the author in the text
   under consideration?

After identifying and laying out premises and conclusions,
you then evaluate the argument by asking: is it false or true?
You may have to settle for a contingent or qualified answer, as
in: it's true (false) *if* or *under these conditions*. As noted already,
evaluating arguments takes much time. Boylan suggests that:

One must limit the number of premises under consideration. The
two guides that should rule such a choice are: (a) the crucial
nature of the premise, and (b) the controversial nature of the

premise. These guides act serially; in other words, we apply (a) before (b). One needs first to examine that premise(s) crucial to the argument. Is it correct or not? If the reviewer is in any doubt, he should apply the pluralism principle in order to help him decide.[11]

The *pluralism principle* refers to the suggestion that many viewpoints should be considered when evaluating a premise. This helps to overcome biases in your team that lead you to look for proof that confirms your established beliefs and to discount premises you do not like. Accordingly, "It is very important that one not allow a strong personal feeling to mask all the possible reasons one might be inclined to accept or reject this particular premise."[12] It is to overcome this bias and to educate by challenging beliefs that teams are asked to argue from an alternative stakeholder viewpoint in the issue brief.

Why focus on a controversial premise? Because it is the one likely to be central to the argument, but not well supported. Naturally, then, it is the one that generates the most interest in those to whom you will present your issue brief — your audience.

But take heed: an accepted premise to one stakeholder group can be controversial to another. You are asked to sift through and sort the evidence offered by stakeholders supporting disparate policy alternatives, not to look for the best justification of your own views. Thus, you have to do *comparative* analysis of premises and conclusions in terms of what is controversial to and accepted by each stakeholder group.

Another model of argument analysis that is quite popular among policy analysts is *Toulmin's model* of argument analysis, consisting of the basic elements of Data, Claims (conclusions), and Warrants (premises). A second set of elements that come into play, but are not always needed in the analysis are these: Backing, Rebuttal, and Qualifier. A pictorial illustration of the model's versions, shown in Figure 8.2, conveys its power and simplicity.

One advantage of Toulmin's model is that such concepts as data, warrant, and claim are easily grasped and used by those who might otherwise shy away from the formality and rigor of logical analysis. Furthermore, the diagramming of data, claims, and warrants, along with the concepts of backing, qualifier, and rebuttal, is beneficial in breaking down the complexity of arguments and exposing their weak and strong points and suppressed premises.

--- **FIGURE 8.2** -------------------------------------------------

*TOULMIN'S EXTENDED MODEL OF AUGUMENT ANALYSIS, WITH AN EXAMPLE*

*(D)ata*
Country X justifies violating the human rights of its citizens as a matter of internal security.

*Therefore: (C)laim*
Country X will not respect international standards of human rights

*Since: (W)arrant*
Country X refuses to alter its position on the human rights of its citizens

*TOULMIN'S EXTENDED MODEL OF AUGUMENT ANALYSIS, WITH AN EXAMPLE*

*(D)ata*
Country X has justified violating the human rights of its citizens as a matter of internal security.

*(Q)ualifier*
Probably.

*(C)laim*
Country X will not respect new international standards of human rights.

*Since: (W)arrant*
Country X refuses to alter its position on the human rights of its citizens

*Unless: (R)ebuttal*
The opprobrium of other nations makes Country X adhere to the new standards.

*Because: (B)acking*
Nations with a record of human rights violations typically have resisted international standards and criticism as external interference in their internal affairs.

Remember that this model allows you to question the justification for every claim made, so at some point your team will have to accept some premises as theorems, that is, as givens from which you begin. Do not be anxious to accept claims; it is instructive and enlightening to question the basic assumptions of stakeholders. They have a stake in making a strong case for their position, which means they are prone to overstate their case; your task is to critically examine the premises in the case, not to rally support for it.

Although it is appropriate for your team to *know* for whom the argument is made, as in: this is the view of liberals, of welfare rights activists, of pollution control activists, and so on, it is unacceptable to *evaluate* the reasoning, logic, and soundness of the argument on such grounds. Yes, you naturally expect stakeholders to make some arguments and not make others. Yet to say: "Oh, the author argues this way because he's a conservative," is not an analysis, it is a label that leaves you none the wiser about the merits of the argument. This is a subtle and common trap for teams, since some evidence and arguments are easily dismissed or given scant consideration because of their source. We urge you to know the source and its stake in the policy, but to be intellectually rigorous and honest, you must analyze arguments on their merits.

## RECOGNIZING VALUES

Values— those fundamental, culture-based ethical principles and preferences of human beings— play a strong underlying formative role in public-policy and strategic-management. Therefore, many of the arguments you dissect are logically sound and have strong warrants and backing *if* you accept the values of the stakeholder.

This is not to say that any argument is as good as the next, just because values are involved in all of them. It is to make your team aware of two things. First, the stakeholder positions you should be most skeptical of are the ones that most reflect *your* values, for your natural inclination in this instance is to relax your critical stance and assume that the argument is correct. Second, it is a rare occurrence in policy analysis where you can conclude that one view is true and another is false. Usually you are dealing with contingencies, that is, under some conditions stakeholder *A*'s position is correct and under other conditions it would be false. Claims can be false, and they can be supported with inaccurate evidence, and you should conclude so when you find such situations. But in public-policy or

strategic-management analysis, it is uncommon for one stakeholder group to have definitively superior arguments over other
stakeholders. So do not set such expectations for yourselves,
the world is too messy and opaque.

## STATISTICS IN SUPPORT OF ARGUMENTS

Before moving on to the creative or synthetic portion of the
analysis, we must give some attention to a common and often
difficult to understand type of argument, the one supported with
statistical inference and numeric evidence. This type of argument typically is viewed as strong compared when to other forms
of arguments, such as argument by analogy. Especially in the
public-policy and strategic-management areas, where human
beings struggle over the allocation of resources, the use of
statistics bears close scrutiny because of the power of statistical
proof, as in: numbers don't lie, it's here on the bottom line, it's
here in black and white, and, you can't argue with the facts.
These are typical injunctions used to shut off debate by invoking
the aura of objective statistics that reflect the state of the world.
Of course there are other sayings about statistics: there are lies,
damned lies, and statistical lies, and, numbers can prove anything.

If you are operating at a disadvantage when confronting
statistically supported arguments, which can be challenging
even to those well trained in mathematics and statistical reasoning, get help from someone skilled in using and interpreting
statistics. Our view is that an appreciation of statistical reasoning is a skill of immense aid in evaluating arguments and is also
extremely helpful in everyday life. Additionally, you may have
found data that you will, for some reason, want to statistically
analyze yourself.

The major point about statistics is that they should not be
accepted uncritically. You should come to fully appreciate this
when dissimilar conclusions are made by stakeholders using the
same or similar numeric data to support their cases, or when
different figures are used for a single variable, in each case
supporting a different policy position. A second point is that you
should not be intimidated by arguments which include complicated statistics; in most instances you can break down complex

mathematics into manageable and comprehensible form. And sometimes you will want to do your own data analysis, either with raw data, which is not summarized or organized into tables or other forms of presentation; or secondary data, which has been gathered for another use.

Space limitations prevent us from dealing with the variety of statistical fallacies that are found in arguments. In fact, some of the materials your team encounters may be quite complex statistically and we suggest that with the *explicit* approval of your instructor, you seek out an expert who can give you a down-to-earth explanation of such materials. For example, say you find a cost-benefit analysis on your topic— a common type of analysis in public-policy and strategic-management— and no one on the team fully grasps the intricacies of the assumptions made in the cost-benefit model. Perhaps the first thing you should do is to consult a book on cost-benefit analyses. However, some of these books only make you more confused, and there is by no means agreement among practitioners about how cost-benefit analysis should be conducted. Nevertheless, one source on cost-benefit analysis that is readable, comprehensive and well done is Mark Thompson's book *Benefit-Cost Analysis for Program Evaluation.*[13] Should this continue to leave you none the wiser, consult the instructor for guidance.

There are several kinds of statistical errors, sleight of hand, and fallacies. Once you are made aware of them, you are more capable of catching them while assessing arguments. An excellent book for those of you not highly trained in mathematics and statistical reasoning is Stephen K. Campbell's *Flaws and Fallacies in Statistical Thinking.*[14] In this short volume, Campbell gives easily grasped examples of how statistical principles are violated in arguments. This book is a handy guide to evaluating the statistical soundness of many of the arguments you will assess, and it can also serve as a guide to you if you analyze any data. Another very readable and insightful book is Sheila Tobias's *Overcoming Math Anxiety.*[15] This book is especially helpful for those who refuse to examine statistical evidence because of unreasonable fears they have about math. A classic on this subject is *How to Lie With Statistics* by Huff and Geiss, wherein you will learn about the misuses of statistical analysis.[16] Finally, a general overview of the uses and misunderstanding of statistics is found in J.A. Paulos's *Innumerology.*[17]

Arguments supported by statistics are persuasive. Analyze the numbers to the best of your abilities, and get help if they are far beyond your grasp. In the process, you will learn a great deal and produce a much stronger issue brief.


## SUMMING UP

You will get to this point as you discuss the arguments and conclusions (public-policy and strategy-management recommendations/positions) made by stakeholders. You may want to make a large chart, laying out all the competing arguments along with policy recommendations and stakeholders, and consider how the arguments agree and disagree on these dimensions. This should bring out patterns or spur insights. You also can include the strong and weak points of each argument and the premises underlying the values of each stakeholder. Further, list the type of argument being made: whether it is based on an analogy or metaphor for its proof, whether it uses statistical reasoning as evidence, and so forth.

Below is a sample of such a chart in Figure 8.3. The point of this is to simplify your data and perhaps to discover new ways of interpreting it. We are suggesting that you ask how the stakeholders' views can be categorized and easily summarized. How valid is each argument and what are its strengths and weaknesses? Now look for patterns or anomalies in the assessment you have done of the arguments. Do some stakeholders ignore or explain away evidence and, as a consequence, dismiss or ignore certain policy or strategy options? Have any stake-

---

**FIGURE 8.3  Issue Analysis Chart**

*PARTS OF AN ARGUMENT*

| STAKEHOLDERS | TYPE OF ARGUMENT | PREMISES | CONCLUSION(S) | STRENGTHS | WEAKNESSES | VALUES |
|---|---|---|---|---|---|---|
| Group 1 | | | | | | |
| Group 2 | | | | | | |
| Group 3 | (here fill in brief notes on the stakeholders' arguments) | | | | | |
| Group N | | | | | | |

holders addressed all the objections to their viewpoints? If so, how well has this been done? What about the credibility of stakeholders? (Be careful here; discrediting a source is not in itself acceptable unless you have can demonstrate that evidence in support of a position is concocted or flawed.) When this is done you will move into your interpretations and recommendations.

For the public-policy issue brief, the team first takes the unbiased view of society and its best interests. Assuredly, there can be disagreement over what these interests are. In instances where the differences are irreconcilable, minority reports are in order.

Next the team takes the viewpoint of a stakeholder group, preferably (for the sake of learning) one most or all of the members do not agree with, and makes the case for that stakeholder group. Or, the team may reasonably choose to take the position of a stakeholder in its own professional area. MBA students would choose a company or industry, health care professionals a hospital, international relations students an umbrella organization such as the European Economic Community. Similarly, with the strategic-management issue brief, the requirement is for an unbiased position of the company's best interests—which may also lead to minority reports—and then develop an alternative strategic scenario, rooted in different assumptions about the contigencies facing the company, and its strengths and weaknesses.

## MINORITY REPORTS

At this time your team will know how much you agree and disagree about the analytic work you have done and the conclusions you are reaching. If there is still strong disagreement among some members now, the option of a minority report should be adopted. The minority report is the responsibility of the person or persons holding the minority views. Its length and format will depend on why and how much the minority disagrees with the majority. If the disagreement is over policy recommendations, the minority report can be fairly short, simply stating and justifying the preferred choices. If, however, it is a matter of interpretation or data analysis that is at issue, the minority report may be longer and more complex.

A word of caution: preparing a minority report is a last-ditch solution to team conflict.  It does not release the holders of the minority view from their obligations to research, analyze, and write.  Nor does its availability release any team member from the obligation of trying to reach a consensus decision.

## PUTTING IT TOGETHER: IMAGINING AND CREATING

Creativity is a peculiar concept.  The more you try to talk about it systematically and logically, the more you run the risk of missing its essence.  Nonetheless, we offer a few observations about creativity, since it is an important component of an excellent issue brief.

The *Random House Dictionary* defines *creativity* as "the ability to transcend traditional ideas, rules, patterns, relationships, or the like, and to create meaningful new ideas, forms, methods, interpretations".[18] Without doubt your team has been creative throughout the issue-brief process.  For example, firming up and modifying the topic is a creative process.  Now, however, creativity takes a central place as you pull your thoughts together and strive to make creative and workable policy recommendations that address real problems.

Despite this, creativity does not automatically mean that you must come up with unique policy options, although you might.  Creativity might be shown in organizing your report, in how you take the arguments apart, or in how you put everything back together.

Do not, then, feel obliged to be creative just to suggest something different or to appear in a good light to your audience (see how smart we are, nobody else would have thought of these options).  Trying too hard can be counterproductive.  The point is not to be creative for its own sake, but to bring your creative abilities to bear on the issue.  Just as the injunction, be happy! cannot be a goal in itself, so it is with creativity.

Rather than discuss what creativity is, let us offer some examples and techniques for creative problem solving.  A well-known illustration cited in many places, including Adams' *Conceptual Blockbusting*, presents the nine dots problem, Figure 8.4.[19] The instructions are to connect the dots without going through any dot twice while not lifting your pencil from the paper.

**FIGURE 8.4  The Nine Dots Problem**

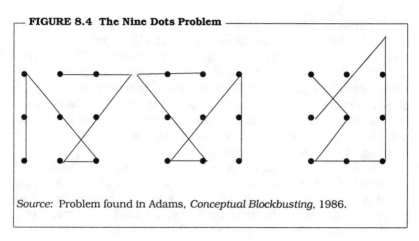

*Source:* Problem found in Adams, *Conceptual Blockbusting*, 1986.

What Adams notes about this exercise is that most people impose restrictions on themselves that are not given in the instructions. They typically assume that the solution must lie within the implied square confines of the nine dots, and rarely think that by using the space outside of the dots they can solve the problem. By confining the solution space and possibilities to the imaginary square formed by the nine dots, most people do not even consider or see the possibility of solving the problem by drawing lines that go beyond the boundary of the imaginary square.

## CONCLUSION

Analysis is the phase of issue-brief work that is both the most stimulating and the most frustrating. It is a tough phase because your anonymous research work is now done and you have to put yourself— your mind, your thoughts, your creativity, your other abilities— on the line, up front, for critical analysis by others. This is hard work, and hard emotionally on many people. But it is stimulating because there actually is a thrill of victory, a sense of pleasure at accomplishing something new and good— your analysis and conclusions.

Watch for high group tensions during this stage. Near the
end of a project like this, anxieties are likely to bubble up from
all quarters: "We don't have enough information!" "We'll never
finish this on time!" "How are we supposed to get our other class
work done?" "I just can't bear one more meeting where we all
sit around and argue!" The fact is that in virtually every case,
you do have enough information, you will finish on time, you
will do fine in your other classes, and your argumentative
meetings are almost at an end.

Now is a good time for team members to be especially
courteous to one another. This is a good way to consciously
avoid nerve-wracking arguments or sniping comments. And
relax! Enjoy the intellectual thrill you get from constructing a
whole analysis, weaving parts together to make up something
new and beautiful.

### *ENDNOTES*

1. David Kolb, *Organizational Psychology: An Experiential Approach*
   (Englewood Cliffs, NJ: Prentice Hall), 1984.
2. Barbara Carlsson, Peter Keane, and J. Bruce Martin, "R & D
   Organizations as Learning Systems," in David Kolb, Irwin M.
   Rubin, and James M. McIntyre, Eds., *Organizational Psychology:
   A Book of Reading* (Englewood Cliffs, NJ: Prentice Hall), 1984, pp.
   36-46, cite from p. 35.
3. Michael Boylan, *The Process of Argument* (Englewood Cliffs, NJ:
   Prentice Hall), 1988; Alec Fisher, *The Logic of Real Arguments*
   (New York: Cambridge University Press), 1988.
4. David Lewis and James Greene, *Thinking Better* (New York:
   Rawson, Wade Publishers, Inc.), 1982.
5. Boylan, *Process*; and Steven Toulman, *An Introduction to Reasoning* (New York: Macmillan), 1984.
6. Boylan, *Process*, Chapter 5.
7. Boylan, *Process*, p. 43.
8. Boylan, *Process*, p. 43.
9. Boylan, *Process*, p. 46.
10. Boylan, *Process*, p. 46.
11. Boylan, *Process*, p. 58.
12. Boylan, *Process*, p. 58.

13. Mark Thompson, *Benefit-Cost Analysis for Program Evaluation* (Beverly Hills, CA: Sage Publications), 1980.

14. Stephen K. Campbell, *Flaws and Fallacies in Statistical Thinking* (Englewood Cliffs, NJ: Prentice Hall), 1974.

15. Sheila Tobias, *Overcoming Math Anxiety* (New York: Norton), 1978.

16. Darrel Huff and Irving Geiss, *How to Lie With Statistics* (New York: Norton), 1954.

17. John A. Paulos, *Innumerology: Mathematical Illiteracy and Its Consequences* (New York: Hill and Wang), 1988.

18. Random House, *The Random House Unabridged Dictionary* (New York: Random House), 1987, p. 472.

19. James L. Adams, *Conceptual Blockbusting: A Guide to Better Ideas* (Reading, MA: Addison-Wesley Publishing), 1986.

# 9

## WRITING THE ISSUE BRIEF

You have researched, and analyzed, reached conclusions. A great collective sigh of relief is well deserved now. Then catch your breath with a short break before the last major and crucial hurdles of writing and orally presenting your work. Typing, proofreading, editing, correcting, and copying for distribution will take a considerable amount of time, regardless of how well you have planned. Furthermore, because the written document has a permanence not found in the oral presentation, try your best to make it read and look like a professional document. It represents a lasting trace of your work.

The challenges in writing this team paper are these: (1) to handle differences in style, quality, and quantity of writing within the confines of the team concept; (2) to write a succinct issue *brief* that summarizes in 8 to 20 double-spaced pages the work you have done and the team's contribution to the analysis of the policy topic; and (3) to overcome the commonplace difficulty of writing, of committing thoughts to paper, that is common even for those who write for a living.

Now wait, if you're thinking of getting flustered or having a panic attack. The organization of the product is already provided in the issue-brief format, both the public-policy or strategic-management versions. Each offers you a ready-made outline to fill in with the fruits of your labor. You have already done a great deal of filling in by conducting the analysis. Now, in the final production phase, you write to fill in and elaborate on each section. Keep in mind that your team may have done an outstanding job of research and analysis, but what counts is communicating well with the written word. Writing is for communication with others, not yourself; the reader relies on the document to understand what you have accomplished.

There are several approaches to drafting the issue brief. A commonly chosen option is for each member to write one section, and then combine the sections. A less common and generally undesirable choice is for one member to take on the entire responsibility of writing. Your choice will hinge on the talents, temperaments, and dynamics in the team. Let's consider the tradeoffs.

## THE FIRST DRAFT

When members write about the portion of the project they researched, the advantages are at least two: first, the work is divided more or less equitably among teammates; and second, each section is written by the person most familiar with it. As for the drawbacks, they include reconciling disparities of style, quality, and quantity among the sections. *One* document must be produced, not a collection of little term papers.

Some teams choose to have one person write the paper, based on the issue brief outline the entire team has followed in research and analysis. This simply means that the notes, views, and conclusions of the team, generated during the analysis phase, are organized and written up by one person. When one person does the writing, presuming the writer is competent, problems of style, quality, transitions, and the overall flow of the paper are reduced or eliminated. The question is whether one person has the ability to write the paper. The disadvantages of this mode are that the person charged with writing the paper may feel exploited by the others and, conversely, the others who are not writing may feel that the writer is shutting out them and their contributions.

A compromise position is for several team members to do the first-draft writing. Then one member takes responsibility for smoothing the styles, editing, making sure transitions are present, and turning the small papers into a coherent document. This method retains the advantages of team members' specialized knowledge, but also recognizes that a single document is required.  As with most choices in teamwork, the best path depends on the circumstances of the project and the skills and interests of the team members.

The increasing availability of personal computers with word processing capabilities, especially if the PCs can interact with a university-wide or organization-wide electronic mail system, is of obvious significance to the team writing an issue brief.  For instance, each member can write a portion of the report and then electronically mail it to a teammate in charge of editing it into one document.  As pieces are drafted, it is possible to keep several versions of the report on hand without the aggravation and tedium of retyping or writing it by hand again.  The possibilities of word processing are many, so use your imagination to make it work for your team if it is available to you.

### WRITING AND EDITING THE FINAL PAPER

It is difficult to write with brevity *and* comprehensiveness. Concise summaries often leave out critical information or over-simplify the complexity of issues.  On the other hand, too comprehensive tomes sit on library shelves, never used by anyone.  You want to avoid these traps of summarization, yet still create a succinct issue brief.  Here are some tips on how to balance on the horns of this dilemma.

The writing style of individuals varies considerably in the use of punctuation, imagery, examples, grammar, and so on. These differences must be edited into a lucid, integrated document that reads as a whole.  This involves improving the quality of some sections, and more often than not, cutting down on their length.  In the same fashion, one section must be connected to the next with transitions, and each section must follow from the path of your analysis.  Having the public-policy or strategic-management issue brief outlines as your guide supplies some obvious points of transition.  Still, take care that lines of argument, styles, and other elements, do not vary from one section to the next, and be careful to show in writing how each section flows from the previous one.

In terms of group dynamics, you may face the problem of having a weakly or carelessly written contribution from a member. If the person admits a writing weakness and is not offended by your offer to edit the contribution, do so. In some instances the writer is offended when others want to edit the writer's work. Once again, your position is rooted in the notion that this is a team project, with a team grade, and it is appropriate to suggest that the separate sections must be combined to form one document. This usually suffices to bring the offended member around, but if it does not, you may have to negotiate the editing process, which is a time-consuming chore. A good tactic is to say in some fashion that the weak section needs *clarification, integration,* (or similar terms) with the rest of the issue brief. (Now that you and all your teammates have read this, you can probably turn these terms into jokes that still get the point across.)

Writing and editing are usually solitary acts. Of course, the editor must share changes with the team, but it will be too burdensome if your team tries to write or edit as a committee. Editing goes much faster, and is also more effective, if one person does it and then circulates the results to the team for comments and further revision.

There are some specific elements of editing we turn to now. It is beyond our scope to give examples and instructions in grammar. Rather, we list some common errors that can detract from the quality and effectiveness of the issue brief. You want writing to serve you, to get your message to the audience. You do not want it to confuse, obscure, or in any sense get in the way of your message. (There are many books on writing and grammar to choose from if your team does not have confidence in its writing skills. A thorough and well-organized one is, Leggett, and others, *The Prentice-Hall Handbook for Writers.*[1] Another good source is Adams' *Thinking on Paper,* and still another is the classic by Strunk and White, *The Elements of Style.*)[2]

Ask your instructors what their favorite errors are, and add them to your list of don'ts. Here are some of our pet peeves, our ten-most-wanted hit list, in students' written work:

1. Know the difference between *its* as the possessive, which does not have an apostrophe, and *it's*, which is a contraction of *it is*. There is no such word as *its'*.

2. Remember that *companies* is a plural, and it is not spelled *companys*. Further, adding an apostrophe to it does not make the possessive form for a single company, which is written as *company's*.

3. Pay special attention to sentence fragments. They are common when writing under the gun, but if you do your proofreading diligently, you will spot them.

4. Avoid using a term or phrase repeatedly, as in: *so it seems, that is to say, considering, rather, indeed, and so on.* Use synonyms, or think of a different way to construct the sentence that avoids your all-purpose terms or phrases.

5. Do not use colloquialisms such as: It was *like* a difficult decision for Company X; and . . . *you know what I mean?*

6. Wherever possible, write in the active voice; the passive voice is too boring and is to be avoided. (See what we mean?)

7. Generally, commas and periods go inside an ending quotation mark, even if they are not in the original quoted text, as long as they are needed for proper sentence construction. On the other hand, colons and semicolons not appearing in the quote normally go outside an ending quotation mark.

8. Don't string sentences together with commas, it's confusing, your reader will forget what you started to say, and things can only go downhill from there.

9. Always reference the words, phrases, statistics, data, or ideas you have taken from others.

10. Don't load up your text with multiple exclamation points, many underlined or italicized words, unnecessary outline markers, and other distracting format features. Keep it simple and clear.

How do you produce an 8- to 20-page document when all that you have done easily fills fifty or more pages and seems to defy further condensation? If each member writes one section of the paper, it is good to let everyone write all that they can on their portion of the brief, and then pare it down later. Asking someone to write succinctly in the first draft is the kiss of death for those who don't write easily; you do not want to inhibit ideas and style.

When you have this potentially far-too-lengthy draft, your team editor can then pare it down with these kinds of guidelines:

1. Avoid *duplication* of materials. Decide where the material fits best in the issue-brief format and edit accordingly. When striking

material from a section, you need not lose it entirely. Merely refer the reader to the needed material in another section (for example: "See page four for details").

2. Avoid *tangential* issues or sidetracks. Place them in footnotes or in reference materials where you can summarize their implications for the interested reader. The use of footnotes represents a judgment about how integral some arguments and evidence are— and are not— to your analysis.

3. Think *laconically.* Ask about each paragraph, each section: how can we say this in fewer words without losing the point we are making? This can be a group task, although you may be blessed with a good lumper (that is, someone who can summarize the essentials).

4. Keep your focus *sharp.* Sometimes the more vague you are on a topic, the more difficulty you have putting it succinctly into words. You may need to loop back to the analysis phase to sharpen your analysis. This is normal, and is not necessarily a sign that the team is in trouble.

5. Can some of the material be moved to footnotes or appendices? In this fashion you can summarize in the text and still satisfy readers who want more detail.

Coming up with a well-written paper can be aggravating, time-consuming, and difficult to coordinate. It is likely to require negotiation and compromise. All this is normal, as too are periods of frustration and slow progress. And when the team looks at their well-done issue brief, you are likely to think that it wasn't so hard after all!

### REFERENCES: BIBLIOGRAPHY AND FOOTNOTING

In this section we consider the options you have for referencing your issue brief, that is, using footnotes and a bibliography. In addition, we examine why it is important for you to do accurate and thorough referencing and footnoting. These are professional mandates and avoid the suspicion of plagiarism.

Earlier, we suggested that you keep a master list or filing system for all the materials used in researching and preparing the issue brief. If you did this, the collation of your references is a straightforward chore that is already nearly complete. If you do not have all the references readily available, don't bail out and fail to include some of them with the rationalization: no one notices or cares about this anyway. Careful readers, particularly instructors, do not like incomplete or sloppy referencing, and they may be well aware that you have omitted essential sources. Should you have to search through a thousand pieces of paper or look up materials twice to get a full reference, grit your teeth and do it. Last and not least, thorough referencing shows that the team has kept a high level of commitment to the issue brief throughout its entire process; this is not lost on instructors as they grade your work.

## Bibliography

Why go to the trouble of having a complete bibliography? A good policy analysis should be verifiable. This means that any interested person should be able to go to your sources, confirm them, and check your interpretations and conclusions. A bibliography is necessary to inform the reader of the materials used by your team and to show your sources in case the reader wants to find one of your references. That is, it allows readers easy access to your sources should they wish to inspect or consult them.

There are several standard forms of bibliographic referencing; your instructor may expect you to follow one of them. When the choice is yours, though, you can choose from styles known as Chicago, MLA, Turabian, and many others. Be sure that the instructor accepts the style you choose. All standard styles are explained in guidebooks bearing their names. Some professional societies, such as the American Psychological Association, the American Sociological Association, and the Academy of Management, have their own guidelines for referencing and bibliography preparation. Information on all these styles is readily available at the library. In addition, most college bookstores carry small handbooks explaining them.

Your team will find noticeable differences among the styles in terms of how easily the team can work with them. If all other things are equal, choose the one that seems most comfortable. Virtually all styles, however, will require the same basic information; their differences have to do with where the information is placed and how it is formatted. The basics you will want to gather for every book you use are these: (1) author's full name (full names of all authors, if more than one), (2) title and subtitle of the book, (3) city of publication, (4) name of publisher, and (5) year of publication. For a magazine or journal article, add: (6) the volume number, (7) the issue number, and (8) the complete date of publication (which may include month and date, or season, plus the year).

## Footnoting

A footnote is a small comment or elaboration on a part of the document that should not interfere with the main text. Here is a sample of a footnote in a main text: "John Dean.[1] who was a high-ranking assistant to President Nixon, was in charge of covering up the trail of misdeeds uncovered by the Watergate break-in . . . ." The superscript [1] after *Dean* is the footnote notation, and each successive footnote is numbered in sequence, either by each section of the issue brief, or throughout the entire document. Because the issue brief is short, it is best to number each footnote in sequence rather than using section sequencing.

The superscript [1] directs the reader either to the bottom of the page or to the end of the text to read the footnote. If you are using a typewriter for your final copy, endnoting is much easier than bottom-of-page footnoting. If you are using word processing, many software packages will automatically calibrate spacing and install the footnotes on the bottom of the page.

How do you know when to footnote? This is a judgment you make about the extent to which what you say fits in with the flow of the text. Returning to the fictitious "John Dean[1]" example, the footnote could read: "[1]Mr. Dean became a lecturer and author after Watergate, see his books . . . and see articles about him . . . ." This is tangential information, yet it is noteworthy to some readers, but to put it in the text could confuse the reader or hinder the flow and balance of the issue brief. By creating a footnote, you give information that some readers want, and you do not interrupt the main text. The manuscript style guidebook you use will give you full instructions on footnoting.

## *ACADEMIC INTEGRITY*

Standards of academic integrity vary somewhat among both professional societies and universities. Even so, there are some widely accepted guidelines covering what is and is not acceptable use of another writer's ideas, words, data, and techniques in your document. Every university has a code of academic conduct; and normally there is a judicial-like procedure for judging and penalizing students guilty of violations. The students among our readers may want to consult their school's codes, or their own instructors, if what we say here leaves questions unanswered.

Our view of academic integrity gives clear and stringent guidelines for using and citing the work of others. *If you use the methods and techniques, if you quote or paraphrase, if you borrow an idea, cite the source.* We have found that some students are unaware of the distinction between their own work and plagiarism— the theft (or uncited use) of another person's work. And we have found a few students who take a who-cares attitude, as though no one would ever read their work. When in doubt, cite the source or author you have drawn from to do your work.

Plagiarism refers to passing off as your own effort the writings, thoughts, ideas, and techniques of others. This behavior is not an example of integrity, because it is neither honest nor principled. We have had students who plagiarized entire papers word for word. In an extreme case, a student actually retyped a journal article, all the way down to the footnote thanking his dear colleague at Harvard University for commenting on a draft. We have seen more students who take a thought or sentence from a source they do not reference. Both instances are plagiarism. Although the latter example may be an innocent act of ignorance, the former illustrates outright duplicity. Some examples of plagiarism we have encountered include:

1. Using portions of another's work and quoting directly with no use of quotation marks, and of course, no citation of the author.
2. Using the main ideas of another author and paraphrasing or merely changing a few words without citation.
3. Citing the source at one point in the issue brief, and later using passages directly or by only altering a few words without citation.
4. Using an idea, method, or technique developed by another and presented as the original work of the team.
5. Submitting an entire document not prepared by the team or which is merely a string of copied documents edited by the team to form an issue brief.
6. Using others' lines of analysis or arguments without citation.
7. Using tables, charts, or other graphic presentations without citation.

The basic rule for avoiding plagiarism is simple: acknowledge what you get from others. If your team remains fuzzy about what plagiarism is, or you run into an instance you're not sure about, consult with your instructor.

## CONCLUSION

For most people, it's fair to say that writing is not a pleasure. Can it be that we were all scared senseless by our elementary school English teachers? Did freshman composition lead us into dumb terror at the idea of putting pen to paper, or fingers to keys? Or did some important someone tell us: if you can't get it right the first time, don't bother trying.

Writing becomes a pleasure when you view it not as an impossible and burdensome duty, but as an opportunity to use certain tools to express yourself. And, when you realize that no one cares how many drafts you write before you say what you want to say, maybe you will lose that no-second-drafts terror that holds so many people back.

Writing the issue brief can be a real pleasure. Not only are you expressing ideas and communicating thoughts, but you are doing so on the basis of well-assessed evidence and sound analysis. You are pretty sure of what you're saying, and you know you have the back-up you need. Further, you have managed your team relationships in a satisfying way, and the final product is a collaborative venture. This knowledge can give you a rare sensation of intellectual and personal achievement, a feeling that you and your team have done something worthwhile, and have done it well.

## ENDNOTES

1. Glenn Leggett, C. David Mead, and Melinda G. Kramer, *The Prentice Hall Handbook for Writers* (Englewood Cliffs, NJ: Prentice Hall), 1988.
2. Priscilla Adams, *Thinking on Paper: A Guide to Writing and Revising* (Concord, MA: Wayside Publishing), 1982; Edward Strunk and E.B. White, *The Elements of Style* (New York: Bantam Books), 1986.

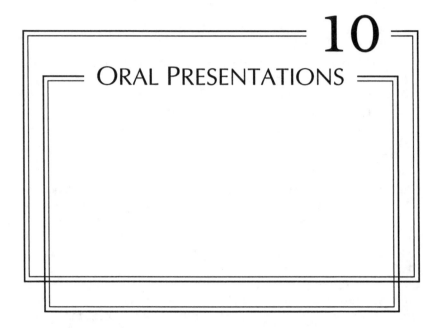

# 10

## ORAL PRESENTATIONS

The written issue brief and the oral presentation are the two media you will use to communicate with your audience. Everything else that your team does is inaccessible—thank goodness—to them. There are some important differences between the oral presentation and the written issue brief, and this chapter will help you to make the most of the presentation.

The oral presentation is certainly less permanent than the written issue brief. However, it has a greater and more immediate effect than does your written work. The audience can only judge by what you present to them, not by how hard you have labored to produce it. Further, a well-written paper does not automatically lead to an equally well-done oral presentation, and vice versa. These are two distinctly different media of presentation with separate demands and constraints. Although the *content* remains the same as that in the written document, the *structure* and *style* of the oral presentation do not. Oral presentations often have a slight informality, or perhaps more correctly, stronger and more varied elements of human contact than does the written document. What reads well on the page often comes across as stodgy and overly formal if delivered orally.

A good oral presentation should be planned, rehearsed, and carried out with the intent of *professionally sending your mes-*

*sage to the audience as effectively as possible.* Although it might seem to you that the formal lecture is the most professional way of presenting information, we do not believe that there is only *one* professional method of presentation. Rather, we suggest that a professional approach has multiple possibilities, given the topic, the talents of members, and the characteristics of the audience.

We have always required a formal written brief but have encouraged our students to be creative in their oral presentations. There is a line between entertainment and scholarship to be sure, but we know from experience that there is an area of overlap as well. Accordingly, we have seen skits, humorous role playing, theme costumes, and so on in the oral presentations by our students. If you choose such a presentation style, you'll have to walk the tightrope between serious playfulness (which will get your message across) and hamming it up (which may entertain but won't educate). We remind our students that their tasks are: (1) to inform the audience through their good research and reasoning, and (2) to hold the audience's attention so the team can make its policy points. Your instructor may favor and require a more formal presentation style, and you of course will follow any such instructions. A straight lecture format can work well; at other times, more entertaining and active presentations may accomplish the tasks more effectively.

## *KNOW THY AUDIENCE*

As you begin to think your presentation through, mentally take the place of your audience and ask how you would like to have it given to you. What will make it interesting, informative, and easy to understand?

When you have some ideas about what would please your team, then reflect on what you should consider to effectively reach the audience: will they understand us if we present our research in this complex way? will they be bored because the presentation is too simple and obvious? are they prone to be particularly hostile or receptive to the argument? Whatever the answers, the content of your presentation will be consistent with that in your issue brief, that is, you can't say one thing in your issue brief and something different or contradictory in the oral presentation.  You can, however, change the emphasis, level of explanation, style of communication, elaboration of critical issues, and so on as you think best, in order to reach the audience.

What if you just don't know your audience that well? Maybe you're in a new graduate program, or you're presenting to a panel of managers your instructor has assembled.  For such circumstances, have a flexible oral report prepared, one that allows you to spend more time on or skim over portions of the report, given the audience's comprehension of and attentiveness to what you are saying.  This requires an ability on your part to read or sense audience reaction as you speak.  Although some team members find this dreadful to even consider, it is not that difficult if you are able to relax after getting started (virtually everyone has stage fright before speaking).  The speaker can see, for example, if members of the audience are restless, reading newspapers, or nodding off.  One team member could even take the role of audience observer, feeding information to the next presenters as needed.

Another situation is the split audience, containing various degrees of knowledge and interest in the issue.  The existence of such perspectives in your audience often leads to lively debate and commentary, and so can be valuable to the overall quality of the presentation.  You can attempt to engage or address each perspective in your presentation, not by pointing them out, of course, but in the manner in which you structure and deliver the report.

### TYPES OF ORAL PRESENTATION

There are several types of oral presentation to consider, among them are lecture, panel, demonstration, audience participation, guest speaker, role playing, and skits.  Your instructor may ask that you follow a particular format.  But when the choice is yours, ponder the alternatives; and do not necessarily shy away from a creative, if a little risky, touch in communicating with your audience.

**Lecture and panel presentations.**  The most straightforward way to present information to a group is simply to speak to it.  The lecture format is handled by one speaker at a time—either a single speaker for the entire presentation, or a series of speakers, each delivering a portion. In the panel format, each speaker normally makes a short presentation, and then members of the panel discuss the issue among themselves.

Lectures are particularly valuable when: (1) the material is so complex that it needs to be talked through by a person who really knows it, (2) the topic is sensitive or when more active presentation styles might be in bad taste, and/or (3) the lecturing team members are skilled public speakers who can hold the audience's attention. Panel presentations and discussions are particularly valuable when: (1) there are several competing views on the issue that can be more clearly presented by different people, (2) each panel member brings special expertise to the discussion, and/or (3) a debate is considered the best way to present the issue.

Here are several pointers toward more effective lectures:

1. Be organized! This doesn't necessarily mean starting at the beginning and going through to the end. It means having a plan about how the material can be most effectively presented.
2. Invest your energy to win the audience's attention. Engage the audience by showing them that you yourself are engaged and interested in the topic.
3. Be prepared to stop and explain, to say something again, or to speed up your pace. Watch for puzzled or bored faces in the audience. Use them as cues to adjust your presentation style. You can even ask them if they're following the presentation.
4. Break up your material into small bites. Use examples, stories, graphics, slides, chalkboard writing, and flip-chart lists to illustrate your points and to provide some relief for the audience. They won't follow you if you hammer through point after point without a break.

**Demonstrations.** When someone actually demonstrates the use of a controversial technology, or how a laboratory process is accomplished, or a particular training device, or whatever, the audience can be captivated and will learn something as they can in no other manner. One of our teams, studying the issue of employee privacy and employer testing, brought in a polygraph operator, who demonstrated how the lie detector machine worked and how important the style of questioning was in the results obtained. Another team invited an asbestos-removal company to demonstrate the safety equipment their workers wore.

   ***Audience participation and discussion.*** Engaging the audience is always more than half the battle in a presentation, and some teams choose to attack the problem directly. We have seen audience participation handled in several ways: giving each member of the audience a small role to play in a skit (for example, the right side of the room are pro-nuclear activists, the left side are anti-nukes), asking the audience to fill out a small questionnaire with results tabulated and reported on the spot, asking the audience to be a television studio audience and planting questions among them. The benefit of this sort of approach is that the audience is likely to feel engaged in what is happening and may pay more attention. The down side is that the presentation may turn into a free-for-all, especially if the audience participation involves moving around.

   Audience discussion is a more commonly used presentation technique, and can be very effective if not overused. If you choose to have your audience discuss the issues you are presenting, keep in mind these points: (1) leave enough time for several people to speak, but not so much time that your presentation is monopolized by the audience; (2) avoid letting one or two people dominate the discussion; (3) give the audience the meat of your presentation first, so the discussion can be more informed; (4) moderate the discussion carefully to keep it moving along, friendly, and productive.

   ***Guest speaker.*** Bringing in an expert can be a very effective way of getting a message across. But if your guest speaker takes up most or all of your presentation time, there are risks, quite aside from the fact that the guest may not be such a good speaker after all. The guest speaker may be extremely interesting, well prepared, and so on, and yet you get a mediocre evaluation! Why?

   If you are operating in a classroom environment, as most of you will be, your presentations will be judged against those of other teams in the class, and most likely those other teams will be participating in your evaluation. Student teams are well aware of the comparative aspects of evaluating in such a situation. That is, they know their own presentations will be ranked against yours. Leaving aside questions of improper negative evaluations from your peers, consider that other teams will look at your guest speaker, look at the amount of work they have invested in preparing their own presentations, and decide that your team has avoided the work and acted in bad faith. Thus, they negatively review you on the amount of effort they perceive, not on the quality of the presentation itself.

Using a guest for a small portion of the presentation avoids this problem. But in such a case, you have to worry about the guest, not the audience. If you invite a busy executive or professional to join your presentation, and then give the guest speaker five to ten minutes to speak, this must be made explicit in your invitation, or your guest may be offended and annoyed.

***Role playing and skits.*** In role playing, each participating team member assumes the role of someone relevant to the issue and presents that person's or stakeholder's views. Role playing can be used for an entire presentation or for a portion. In a skit, team members stage a small play to make a point, but not to encompass their entire presentation.

We have seen highly entertaining and educationally effective role playing and skit presentations. In one, for instance, a student impersonated Michael Jackson and each member played the role of a stakeholder, presenting the issue of copyrights and royalties on musical products such as cassette tapes. In another, a congressional hearing was staged to consider the issue of import quotas on foreign autos; each team member played a stakeholder, and each presented a different figure for the number of auto workers laid off because of foreign imports. In still another, a television debate was staged on the issue of pharmaceutical regulation, combining the serious James Kilpatrick/Shana Alexander style of "Point-Counterpoint" with the old "Saturday Night Live" spoof of that style (Dan Ackroyd, Jane Curtin).

Role playing participants need to act their roles consistently. Breaking role (being yourself instead of your character) is confusing to the audience and detracts from the potential power of a role-playing presentation. Skits need to be folded into the overall presentation so they do not dominate other aspects. They should also be designed to get a message across, not just to entertain.

### DRESSING THE PART

The attire you wear for the oral presentation affects the audience *and* your team. What kind of impression do you want to give to the audience? How do you want to feel about yourselves? Whatever type of presentation you give, you are *role playing* and should dress for the part. Even if you are lecturing, you are acting *as if* you were a professional speaker, which usually means wearing business attire.

A very distracting element in a presentation, in terms of clothing, is an unexplained lack of consistency in the team's dress. Psychologically, the audience is able to see you as a team if you look like one, and vice versa if you do not. To be clear on this: the only conditions under which you should wear something other than standard business attire (dresses, suits, coats and ties) is when the presentation calls for it, as in some role playing, skits, and demonstrations. If there are any doubts about your attire or the delivery style you choose, consult your instructor.

The messages your appearance gives are as important as what you say in words. Make sure that your silent language, of which clothing is a part, supports your performance.[1]

### SOME COMMON FORMAT PROBLEMS

There are several common errors that mar oral presentations but that are relatively easy to eliminate or control, once you are aware of them. Format problems have to do with the subject matter, organization, and writing style of the presentation. We highlight some of these common errors below. For those of you interested in an A to Z review of oral presentations, we recommend Leeds' book *Power Speak*.[2]

**Low content.** It is sometimes tempting to spend your oral presentation time on a single point of the issue brief, thus failing to trace the issue's history or stakeholder involvement or other key aspects. Avoid this temptation by trying to include material on every major category of the issue brief format.

A related problem is the temptation to entertain the audience without making a serious effort to educate them as well. There's nothing wrong with entertaining the audience, as long as they are also getting the content message you are supposed to be delivering.

***Poor organization.*** Organization has to do with the way
your report is structured—what order you use to present your
material, and how much time you give each unit. An otherwise
excellent report (high on content, well delivered) will fail if it is
not well organized. Most teams will organize their report according to the issue brief format in this book, though some may
choose variations on this format, depending on their topics.

There are, though, four basic patterns for presenting material, all of which are at some point covered in the issue brief
outline.[3] You may choose to emphasize one pattern or another,
or to use more than one pattern:

1. *Sequential or chronological.* This pattern is easy for an audience
   to follow. It is used by almost all teams in the background and
   specific history portions of the issue brief; but nothing precludes
   it from being used in the other portions when appropriate. This
   is an analytically weak pattern, but it serves well as a means of
   laying out the big picture or a sequence of events.
2. *Categorical.* Here you create categories to classify subtopics,
   concepts, stakeholder views, or whatever. If the categories are
   meaningful to the audience, this form of organization helps to
   simplify and clarify your presentation.
3. *Problem and Solution.* This technique involves describing an existing
   situation, what is wrong or in need of improvement with the existing
   situation, your *goal(s)* for improvement, and then *how* to bring the
   goal into existence (the team's policy recommendations).
4. *Contrast and comparison.* In this form you present and evaluate
   the similarities and differences in ideas, interpretations of a
   situation, policy alternatives, policy analyses, and so on. This not
   only makes the report clearer to the audience, it also helps get
   them involved and keeps their attention. This format typically is
   used in the analysis and policy recommendation sections of the
   issue brief.

An oral report is likely to have all of these techniques in it,
depending upon the issue and how the overall report is structured. Mixing them is fine as long as the fashion in which you
do it makes sense.

***Poor transitions.*** Good organization takes you far towards good transitions, both within a section as you move from
one idea, concept, or piece of information to the next, and also
from one section to the next. Transitions are best when short.

Despite their shortness, they are not in the least insignificant because they are the conceptual bridges that enable the audience to follow you.

One of the reasons for organization and in turn, good transitions, stems from the audience's need for guidance. Where are you taking them? How can you make it easy for them to see the connection between your ideas, analysis, and conclusions, so that the flow of the report seems effortless and natural? That is, can you show them that this is one coherent report with several sections, rather than several loosely or confusingly strung together parts?

Verbal ways to make a transition, assuming you have organized your material well, include techniques such as: (1) posing a question as you summarize one section by saying something like, "That leads us to a consideration of . . ." or, "How can we understand this issue in terms of the people involved in it?"; (2) using common transition words like *consequently, in addition, however*; or (3) outright telling the audience that you have finished one section and are moving on to the next one. There are also transition techniques that involve your behavior: pausing, changing your facial and voice expressions, walking a few steps, changing speakers, changing graphic displays, and so on. With good transitions, your audience will never be wondering: how'd we get on this topic? as they quickly lose interest in what you are saying!

***Lack of appreciation of the differences between written and oral English.*** Good writers are not automatically good at oral delivery, and vice versa. Some poets are not good at reading their work and some excellent orators are awkward when putting words on paper. It is advisable, then, not to directly transfer the written word into the oral presentation without considering how it sounds when you read it. Speaking the written word can make it sound dry, cumbersome, or too formal. Practice with your teammates. Tape yourself speaking your part. If the words don't work, rewrite in terms of how it will *sound* to the listener.

***Overwhelming them with audiovisuals or failing to use them.*** A picture is worth a thousand words, goes the cliché, and it is fairly accurate as clichés go. Visual stimuli are advantageous to an oral presentation. People in the audience can remember what you tell them better and longer if they can see as well as hear. Sometimes difficult ideas, relationships, or processes are expressed in pictures or graphics with an easiness and lucidity words cannot match. Even simple lists of events, ideas, stakeholders, and so forth are useful to help your audience stay organized. Well-conceived visual aids—which refers to any kind of prop— bring vitality and interest to the presentation. Tufte's book on displaying visual data provides an excellent demonstration of the power and beauty of visual displays.[4] In additon to Tufte, Leeds gives practical tips on how to create and work with visual aids (her work is paraphrased in Figure 10.1).[5]

## SOME COMMON DELIVERY PROBLEMS

A written issue brief contains words on paper. In an oral presentation, however, your words are delivered in a context of your voice, eye contact, behavioral mannerisms, and so on. Close observation of your own delivery style, and practice in weeding out the problems will make all the difference in your confidence and ability to hold the audience's attention. Delivery style problems we commonly find are these:

*Lack of or interrupted eye contact with the audience.* You must engage the audience personally. No matter what its size, imagine that you are talking to one person at a time who is avidly listening to you. To do this, eye contact with individuals is necessary. Not looking at the audience disturbs them, especially if you do things like looking over their heads, into space, at one side of the room, or at no one in particular. Do not, however, stare at one person, or at a few people exclusively. You want to scan the audience slowly and comfortably, stopping to get eye contact with someone for a few seconds before shifting to make contact with someone else. They want you to succeed and you must help them make you feel comfortable; audience-presenter interaction is unspoken, yet very potent and always going on. The audience will begin to relax and listen attentively as you relax, thus setting up a subtle but powerful relationship between audience and speaker.

*Reading a text.* Reading to an audience makes good eye contact impossible unless you are skilled at glancing down and

---
— **FIGURE 10.1  Creating Visual Aids** —

- Visuals should clarify what you are saying. Look through your report for critical ideas, concepts, and data that could benefit from visual explication.

- Write out what you want to convey and then diagram how you want it to look.

- Keep your visual aids elegant, yet simple and easy to follow. Use headings and subheadings as needed to make your ideas obvious, not obscure. Make sure the audience can read the aids, that is, do not write too small or sloppily.

- Use color judiciously to please the eye, not to shock or confuse it. Add color for emphasis and to distinguish points. Too much color distracts from the information being displayed.

*RULES OF USE*

- Be consistent from one visual aid to the next regarding type size, colors used, organization, and so on.

- When presenting, do not talk to the visual aid, look down at the overhead projector or back at the flip chart. Look at the audience as much as possible.

- Do not stand in front of the visual aid or even block it partially for anyone in the audience.

- Keep visual aids covered or out of sight until you need them. Otherwise, they will distract the audience.

- Think about the contingencies for using your visual. Will the aids work in terms of the room size, audience, lights, access to power, and so on?

- Practice using the aids. You need to know if they are awkward or inhibiting in a manner you might not anticipate. Be able to modify the presentation of the aids relative to the on-the-spot factors encountered while presenting.

- Do not make your report a parade of visual aids. Decide which ones are necessary and avoid the pitfall of flipping through aid after aid; this overloads the audience with information, making them likely to stop listening.

*Source:* Adapted from Dorothy L. Leeds, *Powerspeak* (Englewood Cliffs, NJ: Prentice Hall), 1988, pp. 120-122.

---

memorizing several sentences at once. And as discussed above, reading is not the same as speaking; as a result, reading from a fully prepared text may come across as dry or awkward to an audience. At worst, you may begin a singsong delivery that sounds childish. If you lose your place it is likely that you will be embarrassed or even panic. Further, you require flexibility to respond to on-the-spot audience behavior. Good methods of preparation, then, include using note cards or an outline to mark your major points. Some people are able to memorize their report, and some can merely talk it through spontaneously, but a few notes close at hand are a safeguard against the awful event of going blank onstage. You should know your topic and portion well enough not to need a full text, but only the prompting of notes.

***Annoying mannerisms.*** There are several common mannerisms that interfere in reaching the audience. They include:

- Poor posture, slouching, leaning against a podium, standing on one leg.
- Nervous or too frequent shifting of positions, rocking back and forth, moving forward and backward.
- Hands in pockets, wringing of the hands, tapping fingers, fidgeting with papers or notes.
- Arms folded across chest or behind neck.
- Verbal mannerisms such as, *uh, like, you know, um, ah, well, er.*
- Inappropriate voice modulation, speaking in a monotone or a singsong voice.

A fascinating aspect of these annoyances is how unaware many speakers are that they have them. It is difficult to give a presentation and listen to yourself at the same time, so locating and correcting them is best done with information from an external source.

You can practice in front of a mirror or before other people, preferably with teammates, who will critically appraise you. But the best source of external information is to see yourself on videotape giving a presentation. Typically, people are frightened of going before the camera, yet they come away glad that they did and relieved that they did not look as bad as they thought they would. All the subtle and obvious mannerisms of body and voice of which one may never have been aware can be studied on tape; here you can gauge the discrepancies between how you think you do onstage and how you see yourself through the camera. (One of us, after being videotaped, discovered that the camera had captured a mobile face—eyebrows shifting, mouth pursing, cheeks twitching—as other people spoke. Shocking! But with knowledge, the mannerisms are controllable.)

## CONCLUSION

It is routine for panic or anxiety ("I can't do it!" or, "I'll do it all!") to appear in some of the members before the oral presentation. And it is equally routine for the team to work through and channel this seething, undirected energy to good use in the presentation.

You do this by talking to one another so that anxieties can be shared, expressed and examined. When members experience the "I can't" phenomenon, part of this is normal stage fright, something even great actors experience before they go on stage. Reassurance from teammates, practice, and good organization are all it takes to make a good presentation.

What if (horrible thought) the presentation fails after all? This happens occasionally even to teams that are well prepared and good speakers. Failures happen sometimes for reasons that are discernible in an after-presentation debriefing, and sometimes they happen for reasons beyond the team's control. If your audience has just come from the year's most brutal accounting exam, or if such an exam is looming next period, they may not be entirely receptive to your message. Don't worry—failures are nothing more than additional opportunities for the team to learn. And they happen very rarely to teams that have prepared themselves well.

## ENDNOTES

1. Edward T. Hall, *The Silent Language* (New York: Anchor-Double-day Books), 1961.
2. Dorothy L. Leed, *Powerspeak: The Complete Guide to Persuasive Public Speaking and Presenting* (Englewood Cliffs, NJ: Prentice Hall), 1988.
3. Leeds, *Powerspeak*, pp. 35-36.
4. Edward Tufte, *The Visual Display of Quantitative Information* (Cheshire, CT: Graphics Press), 1983.
5. Leeds, *Powerspeak*, pp. 120-122.

# 11

## EVALUATING THE OUTCOMES

Team research, as you know by now, is an interactive, participative process. In keeping with this, your instructor is likely to ask you to participate, beyond your written and oral products, by evaluating the oral presentations of other teams. You also may be asked to evaluate your contributions as a team member and the contributions of your fellow members to the project. Finally, you and your teammates will probably want to hold a debriefing meeting when the project is complete, where you can reflect on your experiences together, gain insight, and release feelings as a team.

For some students, evaluating themselves and their peers is so difficult that they avoid the task by giving everyone the same evaluation rating, typically the highest score on every dimension. Should you choose this avoidance tactic, you are losing an experience that would benefit you immensely in your professional life. Critically assessing your own work is rarely easy, and for some people it is virtually impossible. Accurate self-appraisal can be learned, however, by comparing what you think you contributed with what others think you contributed. It takes a little courage (really very little, when you get right down to it), open-mindedness, and practice, and it helps you learn how to be a better professional.

Assessing the performance of your peers, whether in your team or in other teams, can be difficult for another reason. Evaluating your classmates may cause you to mentally wriggle to the conclusion that you are all in the same boat, and you do not want to be the one who must bear guilt for lowering a fellow student's grade.   Go ahead and wriggle; this is a factor in professional peer evaluation as well, and simply must be faced down. Perhaps your instructors will relieve you of some of this burden by retaining a portion of the grades for their own judgments.  But in any case, your task now is to review and assess your own and your peers' performance in the context of what you know the requirements of the task.

Evaluation means to critically assess something— a performance, a product, an idea— on the basis of relevant criteria. An integral part of professionalism is the ability to recognize that an evaluation should contain as *little* as possible of your feelings for those you evaluate, and as *much* as possible about what you see as their contribution to the project.   The objective is to separate your relationship, good or bad or indifferent, with others from what they gave to the work.  In your professional career, you will be asked to evaluate peers and subordinates regularly, and you yourself will be evaluated.  Separating feelings from performance evaluations may be difficult, but it is essential for fair, honest evaluation.

### EVALUATING ORAL PRESENTATIONS

Some or all of the following criteria may be used to evaluate the oral presentations of other teams: organization, content, communication, logic of arguments, creativity, and overall effectiveness.  Your instructor will give you specific information about what is to be evaluated and how you are to do it, but we offer some guidelines here.

*Organization* refers to the structure of the report.  Did it flow from one topic to the next— that is, was it well connected internally? Did the order in which the material was presented make sense? Reports can be organized in a number of ways, but any organization has to allow the audience to follow the report.

*Content* refers to the meatiness or substance of the report. Did vital questions seem to be barely or not at all covered?  Did the research input seem about right?  Was there an adequate amount of information given?   Or was too much information crammed into the report without much attention paid to its relevance?

*Communication styles* have to do with the manner of presentation.   This is an opportunity to provide feedback to your peers on their unconscious mannerisms and other distracting communication habits, as well as to tell them what they are doing well.   For this criterion, we especially encourage students to write comments rather than merely use a ranking scheme, so that presenters can get as much detailed feedback as possible on the best and the worst of their communication styles.

*Logic of argumentation* refers to how much sense the presentation made.   Were there inconsistencies that were left dangling?   (Note that inconsistencies are very likely to arise in policy research; the question is, how does the team deal with them?)   Were conclusions supported with good arguments and good evidence?   Were the conclusions consistent with one another?   Did the recommendations follow from the evidence, or were they self-serving regardless of the evidence?   As a whole, did the team make a good case?

*Creativity* refers to the novelty or originality of the team's overall presentation style or format.   Creativity does not necessarily have anything to do with the use of skits or role playing, as some students believe.   We have seen highly creative lectures— creative because of the way they were organized and delivered.   We have seen creative presentations that used graphics, slides, or film clips to emphasize points in an otherwise formally structured delivery style.   And we have seen skits and role playing that were not particularly creative.

*Overall effectiveness* refers to how well the team got through to you.   Did they present in such a manner that you understood what they were saying, regardless of whether you accepted it or not?   Was your interest captured and maintained?   Did you learn something new?   Were you, perhaps, persuaded to accept a different view?   Do you think differently about the topic now?   Do you respect what the team did?

## *INTRATEAM EVALUATIONS*

If your instructor asks you to provide an evaluation of your contributions to the project in comparison with those of your teammates, some of you will face an easy task and others will not. All the problems of peer evaluation noted above are compounded when the peers you are evaluating are on your own team. But, the opportunity for reflection and learning are present here as well, so dig in and do it.

Normally, intrateam evaluations will not be anonymous; that is, you will be asked to put your name on it so the instructor knows that everyone has turned in an evaluation and also so that self-evaluations can be noted. But your instructor will probably keep the evaluations confidential, that is, no one else will see how you rated yourself and others. We provide a summary of a student's own evaluations upon request; your instructor may have a different operating style.

Intrateam evaluations are fertile sites for evaluating people on the basis of friendships, personal admiration, jealousies, and dislikes. You may find yourself saying things like this: "I really like John, but he just didn't pull his weight," or, "Shana is really arrogant and unpleasant to be around. But I have to admit she did more than her share of the work and made this project happen." It's O.K. to acknowledge your feelings for peers. In fact, it is positive to do so, because then you have them out in the open where they can be explicitly distinguished from your evaluation criteria.

The criteria for intrateam evaluation give you an opportunity to assess effort and input as well as products and output. It is sometimes tricky to balance inputs and outputs fairly, but this is part of the learning experience. Your instructor will tell you the format to use for evaluating your team's efforts and results, but we will share some of the criteria we ask our students to use. Typically, we ask for a rating of each team member, including the rater, on a scale of one to five, with five being the best rating. In addition, we ask for written justifications of each rating, with reference to these criteria:

❑ Regular attendance and participation in team meetings: did the person come to all or most meetings? did the person actively participate in discussions and decisions? (Note that an active participator need not be a big talker!)

❑ Willingness to share knowledge and skills with other teammates: was the person helpful in bringing talent to the project?

❑ Cooperativeness in dividing the work and getting it done: did the person get along well enough with teammates to allow the task to be done? did the person contribute to solutions or create problems?

❏ Time and effort actually put into the project: did the person pull a fair share of the load? was there anything especially difficult about the person's tasks?

❏ Timeliness of work: all or most of the time, did the person get his or her work done on time? or was there usually an excuse about why the work would be late?

❏ Courtesy to teammates: was the person polite and courteous, or rude and demanding?

❏ Use of interpersonal and group dynamics skills that benefited the team: did the person have any special "people talents" that were used on behalf of the group?

❏ Contributions to final products (paper and oral presentation): did the person stay with the project through its entire cycle, or did the person lose interest or slow down efforts as the end approached?

We normally do not ask students to tell us who did what, exactly, on the project. In the first place, it's often hard to remember exactly who did what, particularly with a well-functioning team. In the second place, we maintain that a group project is a group result, not a batch of individual results. To pick apart the detailed contributions of every team member is to deny the validity of the team effort, and we try to avoid this approach. We do, however, ask students to be sensible and professional in how they weigh relative contributions. Typing the paper, although necessary, is not the same contribution as writing it.

### *THE FINAL DEBRIEFING*

It will be tempting not to meet this one last time. Different projects, exams, job searches, or other tasks will be pressing, and you may not want to spend another hour or two with a team whose work is done. We recommend, however, that you make the effort and have the meeting.

A group project is more than just a paper or presentation—it is a social phenomenon. Over the time you've worked together, you and your teammates have built a small society, task-oriented and narrow, to be sure, but one complete with roles, rules,

rituals, sanctions, and relationships. When the project is complete, the society can dissolve. Emotionally and psychologically,
however, it is usually better for the team to mark its own dissolu-
tion and to extract from the experience something of value to take
along to other small societies that members will help to create.

*If the team worked well together.* The final meeting
should be a pleasant event, a collective unwinding from the
tensions of getting the project done, and a chance to celebrate
together over a positive result. Meeting over a meal may help to
set the tone—pizza and beer, coffee and cake, or one last
breakfast meeting.

It is important for professional people who have done their
work well to hear from others that they have done so. And it is
equally important for professional people to learn how to tell others
that they have done a good job. So, in this final session, teammates
can perhaps say what they saw as the most positive features of the
group's performance together, and may even make specific con-
gratulatory comments to individual team members.

Criticism is just as valuable as compliments, particularly
when delivered in a friendly, helpful manner. A team that has
worked well together should be able to share criticisms with the
aim of helping team members do a better job in the future.

*If the team did not work well together.* A debriefing
meeting can be held to determine what went wrong and how
such problems can be avoided in the future. The final meeting
may not be so pleasant, but the team can and must keep it from
being desperately unpleasant.

There is a grave risk that such a meeting will be used to dump
all the team's anger and frustration on one scapegoat teammate,
who may or may not deserve such treatment. Even if the scapegoat
was indeed a source of the team's problems, the risk is that the
scapegoat will: (1) be blamed unfairly for everything that went
wrong, (2) suffer emotional damage from bearing the brunt of such
a hostile experience, and/or (3) be negatively stigmatized in the
larger group (the class or the work setting). Watch carefully for
scapegoating: if the team begins to focus all its energy on what one
member did wrong, someone on the team must have the presence
of mind to step in and redirect the discussion toward a more
general analysis of the group's problems.

The conflict resolution skills you learned earlier will be helpful here. Another productive tactic is to establish a rule that members must speak only about their own performances, both positive and negative, as someone summarizes each person's comments on a chalkboard or flip chart. This allows team members to see two important things: (1) members can define their contributions positively, no matter what other people think about them; and (2) all members contribute to the existence of a dysfunctional group in some way or another. Pondering these conclusions will take you far toward understanding how people work in groups.

*If the team worked well but the project didn't.* The final meeting should be an intense analysis of what went wrong and how such difficulties could have been avoided. The team will be unhappy about its performance, but satisfied with its interpersonal dynamics. Thus, the positives and negatives of the project itself can be the focus of discussion, with critical analysis offered in a gentle, helpful way so that teammates learn from the experience.

### CONCLUSION

Team research can be a difficult and nerve-wracking experience, or it can be intensely satisfying and dynamic. Typically, as you can probably certify, the experience is something in between these extremes. Most teams have their ups and downs, but most are able to solve their interpersonal and task-related problems and produce a satisfactory outcome. Some teams cannot solve their problems, and in such a case, team members need to pay special attention to *why* those problems persisted so that lessons can be learned even if the project fails. And a very few teams don't seem to have any problems. They stay task focused and work exceedingly well together without paying much overt attention to group dynamics.

Whatever the experience has been for you, it will have taught you a great deal about yourself, other people, how people do and do not work together, and how you yourself contribute to the workings of a task group. Additionally, you have learned something about the process of research and policy analysis:

both the mechanics of finding information and the intellectual work of assessing it, analyzing it, putting it together in a new package, and drawing conclusions from it. Finally, you have learned something about the problems and opportunities of peer and product evaluation.

One way to define the experience is to say that you have finished an assignment and turned it in for a grade. But don't cheat yourself this way—there's much more to what you have done. People, tasks, and products are the most basic components of teamwork. Professionals find themselves, more often than ever before, working in teams. In doing this issue-brief project, you have grown professionally and you have made some important links between your educational experience and the rest of your life. That, we believe, is what education is all about.

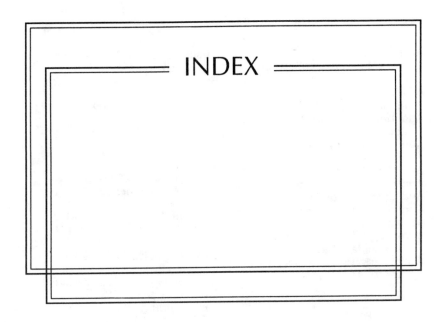

# INDEX